The Matter of Images

Essays on representations

Richard Dyer

London and New York

First published 1993
by Routledge
11 New Fetter Lane, London EC4P 4EE

Simultaneously published in the USA and Canada
by Routledge
29 West 35th Street, New York, NY 10001

Reprinted 1995, 2000

Routledge is an imprint of the Taylor & Francis Group

Typeset in Times by Florencetype Ltd, Kewstoke
Printed and bound in Great Britain by Butler & Tanner Ltd, Frome

British Library Cataloguing in Publication Data
A catalogue record for this book is available from the British Library

Library of Congress Cataloguing in Publication Data
A catalogue record for this book is available from the Library of Congress

ISBN 0-415-05718-3 (hbk)   ISBN 0-415-05719-1 (pbk)

Contents

Illustrations

I should like to thank and acknowledge the following for stills or other illustrations: BFI Stills, Posters and Design (figures 4.1, 4.7, 4.8, 4.9, 4.14, 4.15, 4.17, 4.18, 4.20, 4.21, 4.22, 5.1, 5.2, 5.3, 5.4, 5.5 5.6, 5.7, 5.8, 6.1, 6.2, 7.1, 7.2, 13.1, 13.2, 13.3, 13.4), JEB and Glad Hag Books (figures 4.23, 4.24, 4.25, 4.26), National Portrait Gallery, London (figure 6.3), Centre Georges Pompidou, Paris (figure 6.5), Tate Gallery, London (figure 6.6).

Chapter 1

Introduction

The essays collected here all deal, through particular instances, with the cultural representation of social groupings. This is 'images of' analysis of the kind that has burgeoned in the past twenty years, starting with work on women and black people, spreading to other marginalized or oppressed groups, such as ethnic minorities, lesbians and gay men, the disabled and the aged, and now beginning, with studies on men, to encompass dominant or majority groups. These essays were part of that trajectory.

The impulse behind the writing of them was political. It sprang from the feeling that how social groups are treated in cultural representation is part and parcel of how they are treated in life, that poverty, harassment, self-hate and discrimination (in housing, jobs, educational opportunity and so on) are shored up and instituted by representation. The resonances of the term 'representation' suggest as much. How a group is represented, presented over again in cultural forms, how an image of a member of a group is taken as representative of that group, how that group is represented in the sense of spoken for and on behalf of (whether they represent, speak for themselves or not), these all have to do with how members of groups see themselves and others like themselves, how they see their place in society, their right to the rights a society claims to ensure its citizens. Equally re-presentation, representativeness, representing have to do also with how others see members of a group and their place and rights, others who have the power to affect that place and those rights. How we are seen determines in part how we are treated; how we treat others is based on how we see them; such seeing comes from representation.

The representation of women and other oppressed groups was, and by and large still is, a relentless parade of insults. Anger, despair or contempt at these fuels 'images of' writing but can also block real investigation. Much image analysis seems only to demonstrate that everything is the same and it's all awful. There is something deadly about such reductive work: it tells one little and thus does rather little politically. It is important not to lose the fire of 'images of' work but it needs to be tempered by considerations that get more nearly at the complexity and elusiveness, the real political difficulty, of representations.

This means, first of all, stressing that representations are presentations, always and necessarily entailing the use of the codes and conventions of the available cultural forms of presentation. Such forms restrict and shape what can be said by and/or about any aspect of reality in a given place in a given society at a given time, but if that seems like a limitation on saying, it is also what makes saying possible at all. Cultural forms set the wider terms of limitation and possibility for the (re)presentation of particularities and we have to understand how the latter are caught in the former in order to understand why such-and-such gets (re)presented in the way it does. Without understanding the way images function in terms of, say, narrative, genre or spectacle, we don't really understand why they turn out the way they do.

Secondly, cultural forms do not have single determinate meanings – people make sense of them in different ways, according to the cultural (including sub-cultural) codes available to them. For instance, people do not necessarily read negative images of themselves as negative. One of the first publications to point this out was Ann Kaplan's collection on women in film noir (1978), which suggested that it was possible to be inspired rather than offended by images that had been assumed to be, and probably were culturally encoded as, negative, that there was something exhilarating about the way femmes fatales in film noir give men the run-around and exude such incandescent power. Much work since then has stressed the multiple ways in which audiences make sense of images. In stressing complexity and contradictoriness at the point of reception, however, I am not suggesting that people can make representations mean anything they want them to mean. We are all restricted by both the viewing and the reading codes to which we have access (by virtue of where we are situated in the world and the social order) and by what representations there are for us to view and read. The prestige of high culture, the centralization of mass cultural production, the literal poverty of marginal cultural production: these are aspects of the power relations of representation that put the weight of control over representation on the side of the rich, the white, the male, the heterosexual. Acknowledging the complexity of viewing/reading practices in relation to representation does not entail the claim that there is equality and freedom in the regime of representation.

Thirdly, what is re-presented in representation is not directly reality itself but other representations. The analysis of images always needs to see how any given instance is embedded in a network of other instances. Again, as with the point about reception above, I need to draw back from some of the conclusions that might appear to follow from saying this, even while insisting that it is so. By emphasizing the textuality of representation I am not arguing that texts are all there is in the world, that there is nothing of which representations are representations. This is difficult territory. I accept that one apprehends reality only through representations of reality, through texts, discourse, images; there is no such thing as unmediated access to reality. But because one can see reality only through representation, it does not follow that one does not see reality at all. Partial – selective, incomplete, from a point of view – vision of something is not no vision of it whatsoever. The complex, shifting business of re-presenting, reworking, recombining representations is in tension with the reality to which representations refer and which they affect. This is evident in three ways. Firstly, reality sets limits to what, barring idiosyncratic examples, humans can make it mean. (To mistake a cow for a hat is not just an error in logic.) Secondly, reality is always more extensive and complicated than any system of representation can possibly comprehend and we always sense that this is so – representation never 'gets' reality, which is why human history has produced so many different and changing ways of trying to get it. Thirdly, representations here and now have real consequences for real people, not just in the way they are treated as indicated above but in terms of the way representations delimit and enable what people can be in any given society.

This last point is most sharply suggested by the case of lesbians and gay men. Many would agree that the categories of 'lesbians' and 'gay men' are not given by reality. Most societies recognize sexual relations between members of the same sex, whether or not they proscribe, institutionalize or elevate them, but only a minority have an idea of persons who habitually, exclusively and 'by nature' have such relations. This is an important point, because it indicates the malleability of human sex activity, the possibility of change. But *we* live in this society at this time, where some people do feel that they 'are' lesbian or gay, and often enough to wish to make common cause with others who feel the same. It is true that such identities are never really as comprehensive as they claim – that many lesbians and gay men, for instance, do not recognize themselves in the identities claimed either within lesbian/gay cultures or by the lesbian/gay movements – but it is also the case that one cannot live outside the society, the network of representations, in which one finds oneself. Negative designations of a group have negative consequences for the lives of members of that grouping, and identifying with that grouping, however much it doesn't 'get' all of what one is personally or all of what everyone in that grouping is, none the less enables one to try to change the circumstances of that socially constructed grouping.

The case of lesbians and gay men presents in sharp form what is none the less another general characteristic of representation, namely that it constitutes the very social grouping that it also re-presents. (This is why I prefer 'grouping' to 'group', since the latter seems more fixed and given, the former stresses the business of construction.) Ethnic representation for instance is based not on inevitable categories pre-existing human consciousness but on the organization of perception. To take two examples: to refer to someone as 'nero' (black) in northern Italy is liable to be taken as meaning that the person is from southern Italy; a light-skinned, black-identified friend of mine found that he was treated as white when he visited Africa. Ethnicity is in the eye of the culture. Even the categorical sex distinction male: female (and not just the gender distinction masculine: feminine) may not be the bottom line of how we must represent humans, as Judith Butler (1990) among others argues. In saying this, however, I give no ground to those who say that there is no reality except representation itself. There are variations in skin colour, there are genital differences, there are different sexual practices – representation is the organization of the perception of these into comprehensibility, a comprehensibility that is always frail, coded, in other words, human.

The complexity of representation lies then in its embeddedness in cultural forms, its unequal but not monolithic relations of production and reception, its tense and unfinished, unfinishable relation to the reality to which it refers and which it affects. It also lies, finally, in its comprehensiveness. Women, ethnic minorities, gay people and so on are not the only ones to be social groupings; everyone belongs to social groupings; indeed we all belong in many groupings, often antagonistic to one another or at the least implying very different accesses to power. The groupings that have tended not to get addressed in 'images of' work, however, are those with most access to power: men, whites, heterosexuals, the able-bodied. The problem with not addressing them as such is that they then function as simply the human norm, without specificity and thus without a specifiable relation to power. Latterly the study of the representation of men and masculinity has become a growth industry, but there is still next to no work on whites, heterosexuals or the able-bodied. Such work, adumbrated in a couple of pieces here, seeks to make normality strange, that is, visible and specific. This must not imply, however, an equivalence between such images and those of women and other oppressed groupings. The project of making normality strange and thus ultimately decentring it must not seem to say that this has already taken place, that now masculinity, whiteness, heterosexuality and able-bodiedness are just images of identity alongside all others. That may be the point we wish to reach but we are not there yet. As in all others issues of representation, we must not leave the matter of power out of account any more than the matter of representation itself.

The essays that follow have not been altered from their original publication except for minor errors. With a collection like this it is impossible to acknowledge all those who contributed to the writing of them, but I should like to thank those who commissioned, edited and encouraged them: Sarah Benton, Jim Cook, Chris Granlund, Larry Gross, Tony Harrold, Jim

Hillier, Martin Humphries, Chuck Kleinhans and *Jump Cut*, Kobena Mercer, Andy Metcalfe and Sally Townsend.

REFERENCES

Butler, Judith (1990) *Gender Trouble*, London/New York: Routledge.
Kaplan, E. Ann (ed.) (1978) *Women in Film Noir*, London: British Film Institute.

Chapter 2

In a word

Many people put a great deal of energy into cleansing language. A colleague of mine is tireless in her use of 'chairperson' in the face of almost everyone else's implacable use of 'chairman'. Jesse Jackson has headed a campaign to make everyone use 'African-American', a campaign that seems to be working, at least as far as the liberal press in the States is concerned. It is one of the more astonishing achievements of 1970s politics that queers now find themselves called by a term they themselves nominated, gay.

Struggling over words is one of the most immediate, practical, day-to-day forms of what may be broadly characterized as left cultural politics. They are at one end of a continuum that includes attention to presentation across the board (the cover of *Marxism Today*, Neil Kinnock's suits), the now widely granted centrality of identity as a basis for activity, ideologically inflected reviewing of the arts and the increased stress on the role of consciousness and culture in our general understanding of why and how things are as they are and how to change them. The term 'cultural politics' to cover all that is itself inadequate. In some ways, the venerable socialist reference to 'the struggle for hearts and minds' is better, because more concrete and inclusive, but it had its own drawback. It tended to imply that there is 'real politics' and a correct way, to which socialists had to persuade people (their hearts and their minds) to assent, whereas 'cultural politics' sees all aspects of the life of the heart and mind as themselves political and all politics as emotional and ideological. 'Culture' is not just the vehicle whereby you win people over to something else that is not culture – culture is politics, politics is culture.

There is no doubt in my mind about the importance of this development. It is not excessively sweeping to observe that the overwhelming reason for the failure of socialism so far, from what we now observe in Eastern Europe, is not a failure of presentation but the desperate inadequacy of a politics that was not about where people were at in their hearts and minds, what they wanted, what fulfilled them. Yet for all that, there is a problem about cultural politics and it is well illustrated by the problems of struggles over words.

Insisting on chairperson, African-American, gay, is a drip-drip-drip that we have to keep up, yet there's something unsatisfactory about it too. It's not so much its slowness and the seeming inertia of language but the way there nearly always turns out to be something off about the words and terms we want to get established. We may succeed in some measure in bringing about the change in vocabulary, but how about the meanings and feelings, the minds and hearts?

The feminist project is in some ways different from that of ethnic minority or lesbian/gay interventions. Changing 'man' to 'person' and so on is about rendering language gender-neutral so that we come to see most human functions as just that, human, not male. For ethnic minorities, lesbians and gay men and other groups (the elderly/senior citizens/people of the third age, for instance, or the disabled/physically challenged/ differently abled), on the other hand, it is more a question of getting new terms established to describe who we are. It is this word project that I want to focus on here.

I had better come straight out with one of the things that set me thinking about this: I have never liked the word 'gay'. It's still the word I would use and wish to have used to describe myself and those like myself, but all the same it embarrasses me. I'm not giving ground to those who always said that the gay movement had 'spoilt' the word 'gay', had 'deprived the language of a very useful word' by associating it with sexual peculiarity – those people are very welcome to have back 'queer', 'bent', 'pervert' and all the other very useful words that were in danger of going out of all but homophobic commission. Nor am I going along with the likes of Richard Ingrams, who opined in a recent Sunday newspaper that most of the gays he knew were not gay but miserable (as well any gay man knowing him might be). It's just that to me 'gay' is a rather trivial word, too much suggesting only fun-fun-fun, not adequate to the complexities and varied-ness of being . . . gay. No word could ever do all that, but 'gay' feels like a delimitation, an insistence on one aspect.

The alternatives are no better, of course. The 'homo' words, quite apart from the learned feel where one wants a colloquial term to trip off the mouth, each have their problems. 'Homosexual' is too emphatically sex-ual, with no affective or social ring; 'homo-erotic' is too broad, too widely (and usefully) applied to any libidinally charged contact between people of the same sex (such as fathers and sons, contact sports, men in line peeing); 'homophile' is too namby-pamby, not sexual enough, and anyway never caught on. The strategy of reclaiming homophobic words, turning them disconcertingly back on society, as in the defiant use of 'faggot' and 'queer' by many activists, does not rid such words of associations of oddness and marginality, and only sounds proud to gay men who don't feel ashamed of being queer.

'Gay' has another problem too. Some people use it to apply to both women and men (and I have a sense that in North America this is increasingly so among lesbians/gay women themselves), but feminist lesbians have generally resisted this. However, 'lesbian' instead is not a straightforward issue. I remember a meeting at the Birmingham Gay Centre about changing its name (as was agreed) to the Lesbian and Gay Centre. Most of the men present, well trained or genuinely committed to lesbians deciding for themselves what they should be called, were happy enough to go along with the change. The strongest voices raised against it came from women, generally older, generally more identified with the bar scene, for whom 'lesbian' was the term 'they', the doctors and psychologists, had always used against women such as themselves. One said that she'd rather be called 'bent' than 'lesbian'. A word with such a positive ring for one group of women sounded very negative to another.

This example suggests that there is only a limited extent to which we can make words feel to everyone how we want them to feel. Words come trailing clouds of connotation that are very hard to shake off. Take the history of progressive terms to describe US Americans of African descent. Each new term introduced seemed to break through the hatred and prejudice enshrined in the prevalent vocabulary, yet each term itself was revealed to be oppressive, requiring a new term to supersede it. 'Negro', for instance, drew from an aspirantly objective description of differences between peoples and was adopted, notably by the Harlem Renaissance, in a spirit of 'taking pride in one's race'. It was the way in which one (whoever one was) was positive about African-Americans at that time, yet it was founded on biological notions of race that seem the epitome of reaction now, especially in the light of where racial pride can lead in Aryan hands. 'Coloured' at first sight seemed to avoid this, no longer conjuring up notions of blood ancestry – yet not only did it still focus on a biological difference (skin), it also had the effect of suggesting that there were normal people and 'coloured' ones, as if all people do not share the quality of being some colour or other. 'Black', by ineluctably suggesting the counter term 'white', avoided this by insisting that black people are *this* colour; it stood against the associations of blackness with evil, insisting that black people take pride in their colour. Yet it seems that 'black' too may have run its course, perhaps because 'black' is still so widely used in connection with the bad, perhaps because it too still focuses on skin. The same is true of the socially generous 'people of color' (including all non-WASP groups), which still implies a norm of uncoloured whiteness. 'African-American' is the first genuinely cultural label, but, apart from being such a mouthful, may run aground on old problems about the 'Africanness' of African-Americans, an Africanness in which many Africans do not recognize themselves and which many African-Americans do not in fact relate to.

The histories of political word change seem always to be this fraught. In part this has to do with having to have a word at all. White people, heterosexuals, the able-bodied, do not generally go around worrying over what to call themselves and have themselves called. Having a word for oneself and one's group, making a politics out of what that word should be, draws attention to and also reproduces one's marginality, confirms one's place outside of power and thus outside of the mechanisms of change. Having a word also contains and fixes identity. It is significant to most aspects of who I am that I am gay but all the same it is only part of who I am; yet the label, and the very real need to make a song and dance about it, is liable to suggest that it is all that I am, that it explains everything about me. It has the effect of suggesting that sexuality is fixed, that it consists of clear, unchanging categories, which is untrue both for individuals and for the historical constructions of sexuality. Similarly 'disabled' lumps together all forms of departure from a physical norm, as if these all form one common experience which determines what needs to be known by and about disabled people. We will always feel frustrated by having to have words to express our social identity, even while that social identity means that we do indeed have to have words for it.

The frustration means that we will almost certainly get fed up with the words that we use and see the negative associations creep back in. This has also to do, however, with the fact that words do not necessarily change reality. *The Sun* now uses the word 'gay', but with just the same hatred as it would have used 'queer' or pervert'. No amount of changing the terms to describe African-Americans will change attitudes, as long as material conditions keep African-Americans overwhelmingly in the jobs, housing and conditions fit for 'niggers'. As long as the material reality of a social group remains one of oppression, the word used to describe it will sooner or later become contaminated by the hatred and self-hatred that are an inescapable aspect of oppression.

The limitations of word politics are of a piece with those of the intellectual fashions at the other end of the continuum of cultural politics. Just as left practical politics has taken on the importance of words, of presentation and rhetoric, so much radical intellectual work in recent years has focused its attention on discourse, on the way reality is perceived through and shaped by socially constructed ways of making sense of reality. This intellectual work was much needed: it has broken with tendencies to think of reality as out there, separate from consciousness and culture; though often thought of as anti-humanist in its rejection of moralizing about human destiny, it is in fact profoundly humanist in its stress on the human fact of the cultural construction of our lives. It is a political and intellectual stance that should stand us in good stead against any revival of 'scientific' politics with their well documented inhuman consequences. Yet word politics and discourse discourse run the risk of thinking that words and discourse are all there is, of forgetting that words and discourses are attempts to make sense of what are not themselves words and discourses: bodies, feelings, things.

What we are called and what we call ourselves matter, have material and emotional consequences, but we can expect too much of words. Changing them is a necessary but not a sufficient part of politics. We change the world through words, but not through words and culture – or, come to that, bread – alone. It has to be both.

Marxism Today (June 1991)

Chapter 3

The role of stereotypes

The word 'stereotype' is today almost always a term of abuse. This stems from the wholly justified objections of various groups – in recent years, blacks, women and gays, in particular – to the ways in which they find themselves stereotyped in the mass media and in everyday speech. Yet when Walter Lippmann coined the term, he did not intend it to have a wholly and necessarily pejorative connotation. Taking a certain ironic distance on his subject, Lippman none the less lays out very clearly both the absolute necessity for, and the usefulness of, stereotypes, as well as their limitations and ideological implications:

> A pattern of stereotypes is not neutral. It is not merely a way of substituting order for the great blooming, buzzing confusion of reality. It is not merely a short cut. It is all these things and something more. It is the guarantee of our self-respect; it is the projection upon the world of our own sense of our own value, our own position and our own rights. The stereotypes are, therefore, highly charged with the feelings that are attached to them. They are the fortress of our tradition, and behind its defenses we can continue to feel ourselves safe in the position we occupy.
>
> (1956: 96)

We can begin to understand something of how stereotypes work by following up the ideas raised by Lippmann – in particular his stress on stereotypes as (i) an ordering process, (ii) a 'short cut', (iii) referring to 'the world', and (iv) expressing 'our' values and beliefs. The rest of this essay is structured around these topics, concluding with some tentative remarks on the relevance of what has gone before to the representation of alcoholism. Throughout, I move between the more sociological concern of Lippmann (how stereotypes function in social thought) and the specific aesthetic concerns (how stereotypes function in fictions) that must also be introduced into any consideration of media representations. The position behind all these considerations is that it is not stereotypes, as an aspect of human thought and representation, that are wrong, but who controls and defines them, what interests they serve.

AN ORDERING PROCESS

Stereotypes as a form of 'ordering' the mass of complex and inchoate data that we receive from the world are only a particular form – to do with the representation and categorization of persons[1] – of the wider process by which any human society, and individuals within it, make sense of that society through generalities, patternings and 'typifications'. Unless one believes that there is some definitively 'true' order in the world which is transparently revealed to human beings and unproblematically expressed in their culture – a belief that the variety of orders proposed by different societies, as analysed by anthropology and history, makes difficult to sustain – this activity of ordering, including the use of stereotypes, has to be acknowledged as a necessary, indeed inescapable, part of the way societies make sense of themselves, and hence actually make and reproduce themselves. (The fact that all such orderings are, by definition, partial and limited does not mean that they are untrue – partial knowledge is not false knowledge, it is simply not absolute knowledge.)

There are, however, two problems about stereotypes within this perspective. Firstly, the need to order 'the great blooming, buzzing confusion of reality' is liable to be accompanied by a belief in the absoluteness and certainty of any particular order, a refusal to recognize its limitations and partiality, its relativity and changeability, and a corresponding incapacity to deal with the fact and experience of blooming and buzzing.

Secondly, as the work of Peter Berger and Thomas Luckmann, amongst others, on the 'social construction of reality' stresses, not only is any given society's ordering of reality an historical product but it is also necessarily implicated in the power relations in that society – as Berger and Luckmann put it, 'he who has the bigger stick has the better chance of imposing his definitions of reality' (1967: 127). I shall return below to these two problems of Lippmann's formulation – order (stereotypes) perceived as absolute and rigid, order (stereotypes) as grounded in social power.

A SHORT CUT

Lippmann's notion of stereotypes as a short cut points to the manner in which stereotypes are a very simple, striking, easily-grasped form of representation but are none the less capable of condensing a great deal of complex information and a host of connotations. As T. E. Perkins notes in her key article 'Rethinking Stereotypes', the often observed 'simplicity' of stereotypes is deceptive:

to refer 'correctly' to someone as a 'dumb blonde', and to understand what is meant by that, implies a great deal more than hair colour and intelligence. It refers immediately to *her* sex, which refers to her status in society, her relationship to men, her inability to behave or think rationally, and so on. In short, it implies knowledge of a complex social structure.

(1979: 139)

The same point emerges from Arnold S. Linsky's analysis (1970–1) of the representation of the alcoholic in popular magazines between 1900 and 1966, where changing depictions of alcoholics are shown to express complex and contradictory social theories not merely of alcoholism but of free will and determinism.

REFERENCE

Lippmann refers to stereotypes as a projection on to the 'world'. Although he is not concerned primarily to distinguish stereotypes from modes of representation whose principal concern is not the world, it is important for us to do so, especially as our focus is representations in media *fictions*, which are aesthetic as well as social constructs. In this perspective, stereotypes are a particular sub-category of a broader category of fictional characters, the type. Whereas stereotypes are essentially defined, as in Lippmann, by their social function, types, at this level of generality, are primarily defined by their aesthetic function, namely, as a mode of characterization in fiction. The type is any character constructed through the use of a few immediately recognizable and defining traits, which do not change or 'develop' through the course of the narrative and which point to general, recurrent features of the human world (whether these features are conceptualized as universal and eternal, the 'archetype', or historically and culturally specific, 'social types' and 'stereotypes' – a distinction discussed below).[2] The opposite of the type is the novelistic character, defined by a multiplicity of traits that are only gradually revealed to us through the course of the narrative, a narrative which is hinged on the growth or development of the character and is thus centred upon the latter in her or his unique individuality, rather than pointing outwards to a world.

In our society, it is the novelistic character that is privileged over the type, for the obvious reason that our society privileges – at any rate, at the level of social rhetoric – the individual over the collective or the mass. For this reason, the majority of fictions that address themselves to general social issues tend nevertheless to end up telling the story of a particular individual, hence returning social issues to purely personal and psychological ones. Once we address ourselves to the representation and definition of social categories – e.g. alcoholics – we have to consider what is at stake in one mode of characterization rather than another. Where do we want the emphasis of the representation to lie – on the psychological (alcoholism as a personal problem), on the social (alcoholism as an aspect of society) or in some articulation of the two? The choice or advocacy of a more novelistic or a more typical representation implicitly expresses one or other of these emphases.

THE EXPRESSION OF VALUES

It is Lippmann's reference to *our* tradition, and indeed his use of 'our' and 'we' throughout the passage quoted, that takes us into the most important, and most problematic, issue in stereotyping. For we have to ask, who exactly are the 'we' and 'us' invoked by Lippmann? – is it necessarily you and me?

The effectiveness of stereotypes resides in the way they invoke a consensus. Stereotypes proclaim, 'This is what everyone – you, me and us – thinks members of such-and-such a social group are like', as if these concepts of these social groups were spontaneously arrived at by all members of society independently and in isolation. The stereotype is taken to express a general agreement about a social group, as if that agreement arose before, and independently of, the stereotype. Yet for the most part it is *from* stereotypes that we get our ideas about social groups. The consensus invoked by stereotypes is more apparent than real; rather, stereotypes express particular definitions of reality, with concomitant evaluations, which in turn relate to the disposition of power within society. Who proposes the stereotype, who has the power to enforce it, is the crux of the matter – *whose* tradition is Lippmann's 'our tradition'?

Here Orrin E. Klapp's distinction between stereotypes and social types is helpful. In his book *Heroes, Villains and Fools* (1962) Klapp defines social types as representations of those who 'belong' to society. They are the kinds of people that one expects, and is led to expect, to find in one's society, whereas stereotypes are those who do not belong, who are outside of one's society. In Klapp, this distinction is principally geographic – i.e. social types of Americans, stereotypes of non-Americans. We can, however, rework his distinction in terms of the types produced by different social groups according to their sense of who belongs and who doesn't, who is 'in' and who is not. Who does or does not belong to a given society as a whole is then a function of the relative power of groups in that society to define themselves as central and the rest as 'other', peripheral or outcast.

In fictions, social types and stereotypes can be recognized as distinct by the different ways in which they can be used. Although constructed iconographically similarly to the way stereotypes are constructed (i.e. a few verbal and visual traits are used to signal the character), social types can be used in a much more open and flexible way than can stereotypes. This is most clearly seen in relation to plot. Social types can figure in almost any kind of plot and can have a wide range of roles in that plot (e.g. as hero, as villain, as helper, as light relief, etc.), whereas stereotypes always carry within their very representation an implicit narrative. Jo Spence has argued in the context of the representation of women that, despite the superficial variety of images, they all carry within them an implicit narrative pattern:

> visual representations which may appear to deal with diverse ideas but which are all aimed at women tend to act as part of an implicit narrative. This has a 'beginning' and a 'middle' (birth, childhood, marriage, family life) but there is only minimal representation of its 'end', of growing old and dying.
>
> (1980: 29–45)

In an article dealing with the stereotyping of gays in films, I tried to show how the use of images of lesbians in a group of French films, no matter what kind of film or of what 'artistic quality', always involved an identical plot function (1977: 33–5). Similarly, we surely only have to be told that we are going to see a film about an alcoholic to know that it will be a tale either of sordid decline or of inspiring redemption. (This suggests a particularly interesting potential use of stereotypes, in which the character is constructed, at the level of dress, performance, etc., as a stereotype but is deliberately given a narrative function that is not implicit in the stereotype, thus throwing into question the assumptions signalled by the stereotypical iconography.)

The social type/stereotype distinction is essentially one of degree. It is after all very hard to draw a line between those who are just within and those definitely beyond the pale. This is partly because different social categories overlap – e.g. men 'belong', blacks do not, but what of black men? It is also because some of the categories that the social type/ stereotype distinction keeps apart cannot logically be kept apart in this way. The obvious examples here are men and women, and it is this that causes T. E. Perkins to reject the distinction (1979: 140–1). As applied to men and women, the social type/stereotype distinction implies that men have no direct experience of women and that there could be a society composed entirely of men: both of these are virtually impossible. Yet it seems to me that what the distinction points to, as applied to women and men, is a tendency of patriarchal thought[3] to attempt to maintain the impossible, by insisting on the 'otherness' of women and men (or rather the 'otherness' of women, men being in patriarchy the human norm to which women are 'other') in the face of their necessary collaboration in history and society. (The distinction does also refer in part to a real separation in social arrangements, i.e. the fact of male and female 'preserves': the pub, the beauty salon, the study, the kitchen, etc.) What the distinction also maintains is the *absolute* difference between men and women, in the face of their actual relative similarity.

This is the most important function of the stereotype: to maintain sharp boundary definitions, to define clearly where the pale ends and thus who is clearly within and who clearly beyond it. Stereotypes do not only, in concert with social types, map out the boundaries of acceptable and legitimate behaviour, they also insist on boundaries exactly at those points where in reality there are none. Nowhere is this more clear than with stereotypes dealing with social categories that are invisible and/or fluid. Such categories are *invisible*, because you cannot tell just from looking at a person that she or he belongs to the category in question. Unless the person chooses to dress or act in a clearly and culturally defined manner (e.g. the working-class man's cloth cap, the male homosexual's limp wrist) or unless one has a trained eye (as those dealing with alcoholics have?), it is impossible to place the person before one, whereas many social groups – women and men, different races, young and old – are visibly different, and this difference can be eradicated only by disguise. Social categories can be *fluid*, in the sense that it is not possible in reality to draw a line between them and adjacent categories. We make a fuss about – and produce stereotypes about – the difference between women and men, yet biologically this is negligible compared to their similarity. Again, we are led to treat heterosexuality and homosexuality as sharply opposed categories of persons when in reality both heterosexual and homosexual responses and behaviour are to some extent experienced by everybody in their life. Alcohol use is clearly in this category – it is notoriously difficult to draw the line between harm-free and harmful drinking. But stereotypes can.

The role of stereotypes is to make visible the invisible, so that there is no danger of it creeping up on us unawares; and to make fast, firm and separate what is in reality fluid and much closer to the norm than the dominant value system cares to admit.

In the widest sense, these functions of rendering visible and firm can be connected to Lippmann's insistence on stereotypes as ordering concepts, and to the tendency towards rigidity that may be implied by this. All societies need to have relatively stable boundaries and categories, but this stability can be achieved within a context that recognizes the relativity and uncertainty of concepts. Such a stability is, however, achieved only in a situation of real, as opposed to imposed, consensus. The degree of rigidity and shrillness of a stereotype indicates the degree to which it is an enforced representation that points to a reality whose invisibility and/or fluidity threatens the received definitions of society promoted by those with the biggest sticks. (E.g. if women are not so very different from men, why are they subordinated?; if alcoholism is not so easily distinguished from social drinking, can we be so comfortable in our acceptance of the latter and condemnation of the former?)

In this perspective, and speaking very tentatively, what is striking about the current media representation of alcoholism is its absence. It seems no longer to be identified as a key social personal problem, to be marked stereotypically as beyond the pale of 'normal' behaviour. Rather it hardly seems to be there at all. This may be related to the development of marijuana use as a focus of media/'public' concern – dope addicts are among the most shrill of today's stereotypes. In this context, all alcohol use seems redolent of old-fashioned values, and especially of 'masculine' values set against the 'effeminacy' of 'hippie' culture. To this one would add the enormous financial involvement of the alcohol industry in the leisure industries, of which the media are a key part, and in particular the reliance of television and cinema on advertising revenue (which, in the current legal situation, cannot come from marijuana promotion but can, and does, from alcohol promotion).

If we look back at the cinema, however, it is fairly clear that the alcoholic did serve *to distinguish clearly* alcohol use from abuse, as if a definite line could be drawn, in order to legitimate the 'social' use of alcohol. This includes the legitimation of excessive consumption, drunkenness and other alcohol-induced anti-social behaviour, since it is possible, by the use of stereotypes, to see this as distinct from 'real' alcholism. The question that such an analysis poses is, in whose interest was this distinction maintained?[4]

From Jim Cook and Mike Lewington (eds) *Images of Alcoholism*, London: British Film Institute (1979)

NOTES

1 I confine myself here to the discussion of stereotypes as a form of representing persons, although the word itself (especially in adjectival form) is also used to refer to ideas, behaviour, settings, etc.

2 It is important to stress the role of conceptualization in the distinction between, on the one hand, archetypes, and, on the other, social and stereotypes, since what may be attributed to a type as a universal and eternal trait, hence making it archetypal, may only be a historically and culturally specific trait misunderstood as a universal and eternal trait – it is, after all, the tendency of dominant value systems in societies to pass their values off as universally and eternally valid.

3 By patriarchy I mean the thought system that legitimates the power of men and the subordination of women in society; I do not mean that it is necessarily and simply how all men think of women, although it is an overwhelming determinant on that.

4 It is interesting to note that the liquor industry has been anxious to reinforce the view that alcoholism is a special disease suffered by a minority of the population, rather than varieties of harm, which anyone might experience in varying degrees,

simply as a result of drinking too much too often. A preventive policy based upon the latter view might well be aimed at reducing levels of consumption (and hence revenue) whereas this would be quite inappropriate in terms of the former view.

REFERENCES

Berger, Peter and Luckmann, Thomas (1967) *The Social Construction of Reality*, London: Allen Lane/Penguin Press.

Dyer, Richard (1977) 'Stereotyping', in Richard Dyer (ed.) *Gays and Film*, London: British Film Institute.

Klapp, Orrin E. (1962) *Heroes, Villains and Fools*, Englewood Cliffs: Prentice-Hall.

Linsky, Arnold S. (1970–1) 'Theories of Behaviour and the Image of the Alcoholic in Popular Magazines 1900–1960', *Public Opinion Quarterly* 34: 573–81.

Lippmann, Walter (1956) *Public Opinion*, New York: Macmillan. (First published 1922.)

Perkins, T. E. (1979) 'Rethinking Stereotypes', in Michèle Barrett, Philip Corrigan, Annette Kuhn and Janet Wolff (eds) *Ideology and Cultural Production*, London: Croom Helm, 135–59.

Spence, Jo (1980) 'What Do People Do All Day? Class and Gender in Images of Women', *Screen Education* 29.

FURTHER READING

Bhabha, Homi (1983) 'The Other Question – the Stereotype and Colonial Discourse', *Screen* 24 (6): 18–36.

Gilman, Sandor (1985) *Pathology and Difference*, Ithaca, NY: Cornell University Press.

Johnston, Claire (1973) 'Women's Cinema as Counter-Cinema', in Claire Johnston (ed.) *Notes on Women's Cinema*, London: SEFT; also in Bill Nichols (ed.) *Movies and Methods*, Berkeley: University of California Press, 1976, 208–17.

Neale, Steve (1979/80) 'The Same Old Story', *Screen Education* 32/3: 33–8.

Stam, Robert and Spence, Louise (1983) 'Colonialism, Racism and Representation', *Screen* 24 (2): 2–20; also in Bill Nichols (ed.) *Movies and Methods II*, Berkeley: University of California Press, 1985, 632–49.

Chapter 4

Seen to be believed: some problems in the representation of gay people as typical

THE IMPORTANCE OF GAY TYPIFICATION

A major fact about being gay is that it doesn't show. There is nothing about gay people's physiognomy that declares them gay, no equivalents to the biological markers of sex and race. There are signs of gayness, a repertoire of gestures, expressions, stances, clothing, and even environments (see figure 4.1) that bespeak gayness, but these are cultural forms designed to show what the person's person alone does not show: that he or she is gay. Such a repertoire of signs, making visible the invisible, is the basis of any representation of gay people involving visual recognition, the requirement of recognizability in turn entailing that of typicality. Though not indispensable, typification is a near necessity for the representation of gayness, the product of social, political, practical and textual determinations.

Social

All societies categorize objects, animals, persons and behaviours, and it is hard to imagine how it could be otherwise. This is the means by which societies order the world and make sense of it. Such categories require words and images to represent them. 'Homosexual' and 'lesbian' are only two of the many categories, words and images of sexuality that contemporary western societies designate or recognize.

That much we can, hopefully, agree on. Recent thinking, however, has been concerned to show that while categorization may be a general activity of human societies, the categorization of sexuality is not. It is argued that not only such sexual categories as lesbian and homosexual but also the activity of sexual categorization itself are historically specific, and indeed relatively recent, phenomena. In this view, sexuality is seen to have been granted a privileged position in the explanation of human affairs; sexual behaviours have been assumed to belong to types of persons who perform them, words like 'homosexual' and 'lesbian' thus designating persons not acts; and a taxonomy of such sexual types has been produced, not only in

Figure 4.1 Decor as signifier of queer/gay identity in *The Detective* (USA 1968)

psychosexual therapy but also in popular culture and common sense.

There are a number of problems with this view of the emergence of the homosexual category. It is lacking in sustained empirical evidence and often extrapolates too widely from official or high-culture ideas about sexuality. It is often used in concert with an essentialist view of human sexuality as being 'really' either bisexual or polymorphous perverse. It assumes that because there were no terms or images of homosexual persons in a given historical period, there were not persons whose sexual activity was predominantly or exclusively with members of the same sex. In these and other ways this view of the development of sexual categorization needs further thought and research. Yet it does draw attention to salient features of the way our society characteristically thinks about sexuality, namely, the importance accorded sexuality in the understanding of human behaviour in general and the conflation of sexual behaviour and psychological disposition, the idea of sexual personality types.

Political

'Homosexual' and 'lesbian' have been negative sexual categories, at best to be viewed pathologically, at worst as moral degeneracy, and in either case calling forth images in which such features as skin pallor, hooded eyes, and genital deformity have been used as visual correlatives of sickness and sin. Such views of lesbianism and (male) homosexuality have been challenged, above all by those people who found themselves designated by the categories. There have been two predominant forms of challenge.

One has attempted to alter the object of the categories, to change the terms of what they refer to by shifting from persons to acts. The most familiar form that this argument takes is that people who perform homosexual acts are in every other respect just like everyone else: their sexuality does not imply anything else about their personality. This has been a major plank in the arguments of homosexual civil rights and law reform movements, and it is in the logic of this position that all typification is anathema. The problem was and is that the arguments about homosexuality are very hard to make on the terrain of existing definitions, which do inexorably imply categories and types. Thus a statement like 'homosexuals are just like anyone else' already reproduces the notion that there are persons designated homosexuals. Moreover, the development of gay sub-cultures meant that many homosexual people did participate in a lifestyle, a set of tastes, a language and so on that meant that their lives were, in more respects than the sexual, different from that of most heterosexual people.

This sub-cultural activity was itself a form of resistance to the negative implications of the lesbian/homosexual categories, in that it took the categories as a basis for a way of life rather than as something to be overcome or cured. From this sub-culture emerged the politics of the late-1960s gay movement, with its stress on accepting oneself as lesbian/homosexual, identifying oneself with other homosexual people under the term 'gay' and coming out, openly declaring and showing oneself as gay to society as a whole. These strategies of identifying and coming out immediately raise the problem of visibility, of being seen to be gay. Wearing badges, kissing in the streets were means of being visible, but so equally were behaving and dressing in recognizably gay ways – they brought you together in an act of sharing and they made you obvious on the streets. Typification (visually recognizable images and self-presentations) is not just something wished on gay people but produced by them, both in the pre-political gay sub-cultures and in the radical gay movement since 1968.

Practical

Socially, then, in the fact of the sexual categories of homosexual and lesbian, and politically, in the desire for sub-cultural identification and for coming out on the basis of those categories, homosexual typification is all but inevitable. It also comes to have a practical advantage. Visibility, and hence typicality, means that it is easier for gay people to meet others like themselves. This is most notable in the elaboration of cruising as a major pattern of male homosexual contact. Initially, mere visual obviousness makes it easier for gay men to establish who is gay and who is not; subsequently, different sexual interests can be signalled through a set of dress and other signs, developed enough to be explored semiotically as Hal Fischer has done in his *Gay Semiotics* (1978). In some measure the male gay cruising system would seem to have beaten what Michel Foucault refers to as the regime of the sexual at its own game of delineating with ever-greater specialization a taxonomy of desire.

Textual

Finally, typification has certain advantages in the production of cultural texts representing homosexuality and lesbianism. Firstly, typification is, as a mode of representation, immediate and economical. It dispenses with the need to establish a character's sexuality through dialogue and narrative by establishing it literally at first glance. Dialogue and narrative may themselves be stereotypical. There are conventional ways of indicating in dialogue that a character is gay: certain topics of conversation often function as the trigger for the discussion of whether another character is gay. For example, childlessness, loneliness, a man's interest in arts or domestic crafts, a woman's in mechanics or sports may be used, each implying a scenario of gay life. As secondary characters, gays have familiar narrative functions: a woman's gay male best friend, the threatening lesbian. When they are central characters, there are formulaic gay plots: the tussle between a lesbian and a heterosexual man for a sexually unformed woman, a plot often ending in violence, murder or suicide: the gay male affair that has built into its presentation from the beginning intimations of its inevitably fleeting, and therefore melancholy, quality. Many of these dialogue and narrative conventions may also be immediately presented through visual types, but that is not necessary and is often avoided since much of the dramatic quality resides in the revelation or discovery that a character is gay, or in the teasing doubts and hints that the text offers on the subject. But, equally, this then becomes the subject matter of the text, whereas a quick visual type allows the text to concern itself straightforwardly with homosexuality, not within the formulae of revelation and discovery.

Secondly, types use a few easily recognizable signs to convey not just that a character is lesbian or homosexual but what that implies in terms of a psychology, a social role, and/or a sub-culture. In a shot from near the end of *La dolce vita* (1960) (figure 4.2), we not only at once and without difficulty identify the men second and fourth from the right as homosexual by their dress and hairstyle, but in so doing are also recognizing a great deal else. We are drawing on our knowledge of the very notion of homosexuality and hence of heterosexuality and the whole conceptual system of sexualities that they fit into. We are also drawing on a knowledge of the social forms this takes, of the sub-cultural styles of gay men. This is not just taxonomic knowledge, an ability to slot someone into the correct social category, but value-laden. We recognize these men as gay not just because those are the kinds of clothes and haircuts gay men have, but because that sort of appearance is related to certain assumptions about gay men, especially their relation to gender. That sort of appearance has qualities – the tactility of the sweater; the pretty patterning of the scarf, the carefully adjusted set of the collar, the crimped, set look of the taller man's hair – that are associated with femininity in our culture. We know these men are gay because we see aspects of them as in some sense feminine. This implies a conflation of sexuality and gender roles that is characteristic of gay types; I shall return to this point below. What I want to stress here is the way in which such small details of an image can so quickly and assuredly summon up such a breadth of social implication, can condense such a wealth of meaning and knowledge (cf. Perkins 1979).

Finally, types keep the fact of a character's gayness clearly present before us throughout the text. This has the disadvantage that it tends to reduce everything about that character to his/her sexuality. It has the advantage that it never allows the text to closet her or him, and it thus

Queer View

Figure 4.2 La dolce vita (Italy 1960)

allows gay sub-cultural perspectives to be always present in a scene. For gay readers and audiences, in particular, this allows a place in the text from which to view the proceedings.

The prevalent fact of gay typification is determined by the importance of a social category whose members would be invisible did they and the culture not provide lifestyle signs with which to make recognition possible. It should be added that it is probable that most gay people are for most of their lives in fact invisible. Acting and dressing gay may be only an evening or weekend activity; in particular, it may not be practised at the workplace, or for married gays at home either. Equally, many people who are homosexual may never identify with the various gay lifestyles, never, in this sense, define and produce themselves as gay.

SEXUALITY/GENDER/BIOLOGY/NATURE

The majority of gay types signify gay sexuality through signs that also have gender connotations. Gay types are thus bound up in this double way with notions of the natural, whether these be cast more within biological discourses or more within romantic traditions of perceiving nature.

That this should be so is hardly surprising since our notions of both sexuality itself and sexual variations are themselves biological. I mean this in the loosest sense, that ideas about human sexuality have been insistently organized in terms of what is given by nature, by what John Gagnon and John Simon refer to as the notion of a 'basic biological mandate' (Gagnon and Simon 1973), whether that be the urge to reproduce or the need for orgasm or the drive for sexual release. A major aspect of this biological view of sexuality has been the attempt to determine and differentiate male and female sexualities, so that not only are sex and gender conflated (biological sex being deemed to produce psychological gender dispositions), but so are sex and sexuality, there being a sexuality appropriate to the two biologically distinct sexes. Although these sexualities have been predominantly defined in terms of heterosexuality, they have perhaps more importantly been defined in terms of male and female sexual predispositions, of which the active male drive and the passive female receptivity are the most familiar examples. Thus it is not the act of heterosexual intercourse that makes someone heterosexual, but one or another psychosexual predisposition which is heterosexual only in the sense that an active drive and a passive receptivity are seen to be inherently complementary.

For various reasons this kind of thinking, although at the level of common sense undoubtedly still dominant today, has been roundly rejected in many quarters. The case against it can be made on the grounds of the anthropological and historical evidence of the enormous differences in the construction of both gender and sexuality in other cultures and other times, but the force of the rejection is above all political. In part it springs from a rejection of all models that root understanding of human society so firmly in the biological. Not only sex and sexuality but also race are all biologically based notions that have historically been used in infamously destructive ways, of which the Nazi designation of biologically inferior peoples (races and sexualities) and medical experimentation on them is only the most obscene. The sexist bias in biological theories of sex and sexuality was very clearly demonstrated by feminist writing in the late 1960s and early 1970s. More recently, the work of Michel Foucault has been influential in spreading the idea that sexuality, precisely by its intimate and apparently biologically given character, is the aspect of human lives that is most open to the exercise of power relations in modern society, that it is through the regulation of our bodies in the regime of sexuality that we are controlled.

In general I would share the emphases of all these arguments, but it is important to recognize that arguments from biology are not necessarily and always reactionary. If a major assumption of many biological arguments is that what can be shown to be natural must be accepted as a proper part of human life, then it is not surprising that those arguing for the rights of gay people have often sought to show that gayness too is natural: hence, on the one hand, the attempt by campaigners like Edward Carpenter and Magnus Hirschfeld to show that gays are a third or intermediate sex or, on the other, the importance of the rhetoric of naturalness in much contemporary lesbian art. Though there is a culturally very significant shift here from a more biological to a more romantic–naturalist world-view, both are arguing for the rights of gay people from a model of nature. It is their conception of nature that is different, not the form of the argument.

ANOTHER ARGUMENT, ANOTHER TYPE: THE CLASSICAL MODEL

Other kinds of argument are possible, hence other sets of types, although those based on biology/nature have proved most successful in our time. One alternative argument has been drawn from classical example. If in relation to female homosexuality this has largely been confined, as far as I can see, potently to the use of the words 'lesbian' and 'sapphic', in relation to male homosexuality it has produced, in addition to the rhetoric of which Wilde's 'love that dare not speak its name' speech is the most celebrated example, a particular range of visual images.

The classical example could be for men a way of representing desire, both in the sense of imaging it to themselves and in the sense of arguing for it to the world; it could be both the form of desire and the defence of it. This inspiration from classical antiquity, which is of course based on the

Figure 4.3 Classical costume ball at Stefan George's, n.d. From Robert Boehringer, *Mein Bild von Stefan George*, Düsseldorf (1967), 89

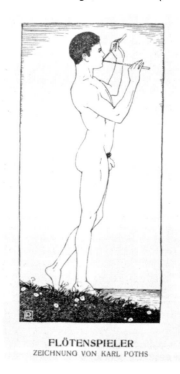

FLÖTENSPIELER
ZEICHNUNG VON KARL POTHS

Figure 4.4 Classical imagery from *Der Eigene*, n.d.

JIMMY SOUTH

Figure 4.5 Classical imagery in (probably) British gay physique magazine, mid-1960s

nineteenth-century understanding of the classical, is classical in two senses. Firstly, it invokes the period of classical antiquity as an unquestionable touchstone of the finest achievements of the human race – if gayness can be shown to be characteristic of the classical age, then how can it be condemned now? Secondly, the argument is itself classical rather than romantic or biological in so far as it is based on the notion of the ideal example to be followed, rather than on what is given in nature. It has thus the character of a moral argument rather than a rational or pragmatic one. The types that derive from it are not only available for formal and defensive representation but bathe both in a morally idealistic glow.

The costume balls of Stefan George, whose fame as a poet ensured that

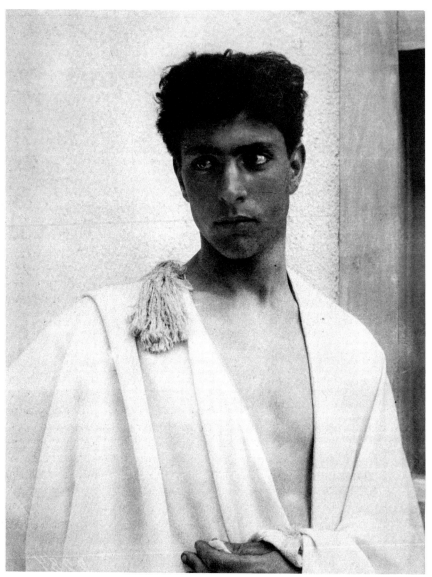

Figure 4.6 Classical portrait by Wilhelm von Gloeden

they became widely known (if as much through ridicule as emulation), were in their adoption of Greek and Roman garb and props (figure 4.3) both rituals of desire – as balls generally are – and the enactment of a homosexual ideal that had something of the force of propaganda. Some of the earliest gay rights publications, such as *Der Eigene* (first published in 1896), used classical motifs so that they both argued for gayness and provided their readers with attractive embodiments of gay desire (see figure 4.4); but also soft male gay pornography has often used classical reference, both in the poses of the models and in the use of vaguely classical props (figure 4.5). Among the most celebrated images of this kind are the photographs of Wilhelm von Gloeden (figure 4.6) which not only use classical poses and props and quite literally bathe the subjects in a pure 'classical' light but also concentrate on the adolescent male, the ephebe supposedly so central to the classical construction of homosexuality.

Despite the coherence and appeal of this tradition, however, it has largely been superseded in gay cultural production, and has never been widespread in the dominant representation of homosexuality. This is due in part perhaps to its proselytizing dimension, but more centrally to the fact that arguments from (moral and aesthetic) ideals have little force in our culture compared to arguments from biology/nature. It is these that predominate in both mainstream and gay sub-cultural homosexual types.

FOUR TYPES

I want to describe here four predominant gay types. Obviously these do not exhaust the range of gay types in the culture. They illustrate two themes already discussed: the importance of gender and of biology/nature in gay representation, and the pressure from both dominant and sub-cultural forces to produce gay types. One aspect of the latter that emerges is the way in which the same types may have different meanings and functions in mainstream and sub-cultural contexts. Two further points may be noted. As mentioned in discussing the use of the argument from classical example, gay types may be both the form of desire and a defence of it; further, they may embody both what it is like to be gay and what it is gay people find attractive – gay types can embody both the subject and the object of desire. Finally, it is clear that any gay type will inflect and articulate other traditions of representation in the culture as a whole. Ideas of sexuality and gender, biological and romantic conceptions of nature are such traditions, as are, for example, bodies of religious and secular myth. Gay types are always caught up in the total web of the system of cultural meanings; what they mean has in part to be understood through this web of meanings.

Most of my examples are drawn from films, though I shall make reference to other media. This is partly because films are my particular area of competence, but the cinema has probably been more significant as a central definer of sexualities than any other cultural institution in our

Figure 4.7 Two kinds of dyke (and one femme) in *The Killing of Sister George* (GB 1969)

century, including television, where the representation of sexuality has been severely restricted. Many of the examples discussed are production stills, not frame enlargements; they are photographs taken on set during production, deliberately posed for the still photographer and intended for use in publicizing and marketing the film. They are interesting because they are produced and selected for use with the aim of suggesting or even summing up the entire film or an aspect of the film. In this sense they are even more liable to lean heavily on typification in order to convey an idea of homosexuality than the film itself may have been. Equally, in their wide availability and reproduction, they may fix the gay type more definitively for the viewer than the memory of the film itself does.

In-betweenism

Probably the most familiar gay types are the queen and the dyke. Although I shall designate them thus singly, there are any number of variations on each. This production still from *The Killing of Sister George* (1969) (figure 4.7) shows, as the film does, two versions of the dyke type – both with cropped hair and wearing mannish clothes, but George/June at the back is in tweeds, has a more fully masculine cut to her suit, and uses no makeup, whereas Mercy Crofts in the centre wears a bright red (primary not pastel colours being more 'masculine') dress with a more 'feminine' rounded collar and makeup which is, however, applied with expert, military precision, giving her face a hard-edged look. Both are dyke types, though Mercy is the more ambivalent as befits her role in the film. Both types connote different notions of masculinity: tweed suggests traditional, rural, rough masculinity, whereas Mercy Crofts's appearance suggests the modern, professional, business milieu. Both, however, also connote the upper middle class. Elsewhere in the film, in the sequence at the Gateways Club, other more working-class dyke types are present. Similarly, there are many variations on the queen type, and these often inflect other values – whether, for instance, of aesthetic sensibility, as in the contrast between a queen working in the trivial art of fashion (see figure 4.8) and the exquisite aestheticism of Sebastian in *Suddenly Last Summer* (1957), or else of ethnic difference, as in the contrast between the two examples just mentioned and Lindy in *Car Wash* (1976) (figure 4.9). I do not intend, however, to offer an exhaustive taxonomy of the inflections of the dyke and queen types; my purpose here is simply to indicate that each is a type found in many well-established variations which cross with other social and cultural types and value systems.

The queen and the dyke both represent homosexuality through what is assumed to be a gender correlation – that is, both are represented as if their sexuality means that they are in between the two genders of female and male. Thus dykes are mannish, queens effeminate. The examples already

Figure 4.8 Fashion queen: *Irene* (USA 1926)

Figure 4.9 Black queen: *Car Wash* (USA 1976)

Figure 4.10 Hirschfeld's typology: the heterosexual male

Figure 4.11 Hirschfeld's typology: the heterosexual female

Figure 4.12 Hirschfeld's typology: the intermediate sex

Figure 4.13 Romaine Brooks, *Self Portrait*, 1923

Figure 4.14 *Blood Money* (USA 1933)

Figure 4.15 She died a bachelor: Garbo as *Queen Christina*

cited, from *La dolce vita* and *The Killing of Sister George*, illustrate this directly.

We are familiar with the use of these types as put-downs. The form this often takes is the tag that gay men and lesbians are not 'real men' and 'real women', which expresses the assumption that true masculinity and femininity are in large measure defined in heterosexual sexuality. However, this negative use of the types should not blind us to the fact that ideas of in-betweenism have been used by gay people themselves, not only in subcultural practices but in historically progressive activism. The arguments of Magnus Hirschfeld were very directly based on ideas of gay people as a biologically intermediate sex, and he had photos to prove it (see figures 4.10, 4.11, 4.12). Equally, figures like Radclyffe Hall, Romaine Brooks

Figure 4.16 Quentin Crisp, real-life effeminate homosexual, from *Jeremy* 1(4) (1969)

and Una, Lady Troubridge, both in their own publicly prominent adoption of a dyke style and in Brooks's reproduction of them in her painting (see figure 4.13), were proclaiming an in-betweenist lesbian lifestyle in a defiant, declamatory fashion. It is clear where the aristocratic dyke in the 1933 film *Blood Money* (figure 4.14) gets her style from, and equally why a gay following has accrued to stars prepared to appear as Garbo did in *Queen Christina* (1933) (figure 4.15) or Dietrich in her films with von Sternberg. This was not only important in its time but has been important in the reclamation of our history, which has stemmed from the development of the post 1960s gay movement. A queen figure like Quentin Crisp (figure 4.16) becomes crucial here; his life as an 'out' effeminate homosexual is seen as exhibiting exemplary courage in his visual display of himself as a queen before coming out became an established strategy of the gay movement. The enshrinement of this in an acclaimed television film put queenliness in the mass public eye, and at the same time he became a focus for debate about the value of the role, its progressive force for us now. This legacy of the queen (or sissy) type, as of the dyke (or butch lesbian) type, is both challenging and confusing to contemporary gay political thought.

I have referred to the queen and dyke types as effeminate and mannish, and much of the force of the image is that gay men and lesbians are, by virtue of their sexuality, in some sense more like the biologically opposite sex. Yet they are not exactly masculine or feminine either. In gay usage, they may be an assertion of in-betweenism or more generally of a refusal of rigid sex role-playing; but in their use within the dominant culture they are more characteristically portrayed as people who in failing, because of not being heterosexual, to be real women or men, at the same time fail to be truly masculine or feminine in other ways – dykes are unwomanly but fall short of being truly masculine; queens are unmanly and unwomanly. Both are thus often seen as tragic, pathetic, wretched, despicable, comic or ridiculous figures.

This calls forth the violent and melancholy narratives suggested above, and with it certain predominant inflections of the types. This is particularly elaborated with the dyke, who is frequently represented as dangerous and threatening. It is remarkable how often she is shown positioned in the same ways behind the sexually indeterminate (i.e., she might 'go either way') woman (see figures 4.17, 4.18, 4.19). In this pose she appears to be trying to draw the indeterminate woman into her thrall, not by direct assault or honest seduction but by stealth. This image of

Figure 4.17 Lesbian stealth: *Roma città aperta* (Italy 1945)

malignant lesbian power is explored still further in the use of lesbianism in the vampire film, where sexual power through stealth, the very heart of the vampire myth, may be articulated with other aspects of fears and taboos concerning women, including the imagery of blood as both sexual juices and menstrual flow. Although undoubtedly intended as negative represen-tations, the very force and vividness of these evocations of female/lesbian power mean that films such as *Daughters of Darkness* (1970) or *Blood Beast Terror* (1967) might be appropriated as almost radical lesbian femi-nist films.

In-betweenism probably remains the most familiar and widespread gay typology. In its tragic and violent modes it reinforces negative views of gay sexuality; in its representation of the nastiness or ridiculousness of not being really one sex or the other, it serves to maintain the notion of rigid gender role differentiation. Yet it may also, through a paradoxical inver-sion, embody a rejection of those roles.

Figure 4.18 Lesbian stealth: *Huis clos* (France 1954)

Figure 4.19 Lesbian stealth: *Lust for a Vampire* (GB 1970)

Macho

In *The Boys in the Band* (1970) one of the characters is given a macho-style hustler as a birthday present (figure 4.20) – his exaggeratedly masculine style contrasts with the varieties of queens and sad young men who make up the rest of the cast. By the time of *A Different Story* (1978), however, the gay man is himself identified by his macho look (figure 4.21). It is an exaggerated masculinity, and indeed its very exaggeratedness marks it off from the conventional masculine look on which it is based. It is, moreover, a consciously erotic look. The practical, instrumental connotations of working-class male clothing are transformed into pure signs of eroticism. The typing of the Perry King character in the still is precise – the stance draws the eye to the crotch; the t-shirt is stretched not only to reveal body

Figure 4.20 Macho man as gift for a gay man: *The Boys in the Band* (USA 1970)

Figure 4.21 Gay man as macho man: *A Different Story* (USA 1978)

contours but to become a tactile surface in its own right; the hair is not just neat but clean as well with the light catching it so that the viewer might wish to run her/his fingers through it.

In marking off the macho man from the simply straight man, this gay type retains the idea of (male) homosexuality implying something different in relation to gender, but here there is no notion of a biological in-betweenism but an excess of masculinity. However, whereas in-betweenism is predominantly conceptualized in relation to biological androgyny, macho is far more clearly the conscious deployment of *signs* of masculinity. In this way macho is close to the other predominant forms of gay male ghetto culture, camp and drag. The latter may be read within the idea of in-betweenism, the queen being, after all, camp in behaviour and given to wearing women's clothes. But there is a difference between camp behaviour and a camp attitude. The latter implies an ironic stance towards official or mainstream images or representations. Camp in this sense is profoundly denaturalizing. Far from expressing a sense of what is natural, it constantly draws attention to the artifices attendant on the construction of images of what is natural. Camp, drag and macho self-consciously play the signs of gender, and it is in the play and exaggeration that an alternative sexuality is implied – a sexuality, that is, that recognizes itself as in a problematic relationship to the conventional conflation of sexuality and gender.

The sad young man[1]

In the 1950s and 1960s it was easy to spot the emergent and still rare gay novel by its cover. Clean-shaven, young models are lit in ways that both soften their features and also suggest a twilight existence, with all the melancholy associations that twilight has in our culture. Neither man manages directly to catch the other's eye: either one gazes and the other looks thoughtfully (troubledly?) away, or else both look over their shoulders towards but not at each other. Thus everything is young, soft, half-lit, half-establishing contact, but frozen at that moment, at the moment of yearning. They are 'sad young men'.

The sad young man is neither androgynously in-between the genders nor playing with the signs of gender. His relationship to masculinity is more difficult, and thus sad. He is a young man, hence not yet really a real man. He is soft; he has not yet achieved assertive masculine hardness. He is also physically less than a man. In many paperback covers he does not hold his head up but hangs it. There is perhaps an echo in the stance of the major source of this imagery, the Judeo-Christian tradition. The sad young man is a martyr figure.

Christ was a young man on the cross; he is also the most familiar image of a man in western culture. The crucifix sets the characteristic Christian

Figure 4.22 Fireworks (USA 1947)

register of aesthetic response, adoration of a man in pain. Subsequent martyr figures, especially St Sebastian, have developed this register and have also been the occasion for the representation of male beauty. Once again conflating subject and object of homosexual desire, the sad young man embodies a mode of sexuality we might now label masochistic. Not simply despite but because of the history of Christian persecution of gays, the Christian tradition yields an iconography of punishment as pleasure, suffering as beauty, that has been particularly fruitful in the development of gay images.

It is explored in the film *Fireworks* (1347). The central motif of the film is a photograph of a sailor holding a young man in his arms in a stance that is a visual rhyme with the Christian *pietà* (figure 4.22). This photograph, often used to evoke the film and the filmic world of its director, Kenneth Anger, is in itself an image of masochistic homosexual desire. In the film it is looked at by the young man and thus represents his memory or fantasy. (The fact that it is a photograph does not mean in the logic of this film that it represents an event that has actually taken place.) Thus an image of gay desire is also an image of what the gay person is. The face of the young man, in its soft, troubled expression, is an icon of beautiful melancholy found equally, for instance, in the book covers, in an even earlier avant-garde film, *Lot in Sodom* (1930), and in such gay identification figures as Montgomery Clift and Dirk Bogarde.

Lesbian feminism

The film *Word Is Out* (1977) registers a difference between contemporary lesbian and gay male lifestyles. Though concerned to present a range of gay people, and in some ways setting itself against the notion of typicality, the film none the less marks a broad distinction between a gay male culture that tends toward artifice and a lesbian culture that tends toward naturalness. The film's musical interludes show this most clearly, not only in the kind of music but in the visual presentation of it. The gay male music is disco, clearly related to Tamla in the accompanying visual production, the line-up of singers following a set routine dressed in identical, showbizzy, sexy clothes. The lesbian music is folk-related, with all that that connotes of ideas of natural music; the singers each accompany themselves on a guitar, a simple, widely available instrument, and do not appear to perform to an audience, as the male group does, but as it were for themselves. Nor are the signs of self-presentation marked as with the men – no makeup, non-showbiz clothes, indeed checked shirts and jeans that themselves carry rural, naturalistic connotations.

This tendency of lesbian cultural production can be seen elsewhere. The book *Eye to Eye: Portraits of Lesbians* (1979) by JEB is particularly interesting here. Did one not have the title of the book, one would not necessarily interpret photographs like these as lesbian. Yet one does have the title, it is part of the meaning of the photos, and the title renders the lesbianism of the photos visible. The majority of the photos deploy a rhetoric of the natural, in their largely direct (apparently transparent), eye-level approach and in their iconography of, for instance, ethnic or sub-hippie dress, practical, hands-on-tools crafts (figure 4.23), even where the technology itself is quite highly developed (figure 4.24), and in their use of nature itself (figure 4.25).

This series of photographs, or, for example, the films of Barbara Hammer with their extensive use of flower imagery, is neither an asser-tion of in-betweenism nor a play on the signs of the natural. A further example from JEB (figure 4.26) with its caption illustrates most clearly what is involved. It is a representation of lesbianism as a femininity that is almost pantheistic in origin. It refuses the analytical, taxonomic appro-priation of nature that the institution of biology has promulgated, and in this sense it is close to the kind of romantic receptivity to nature of the hippie movement, to which JEB's and Hammer's work is visually quite close. This is, however, crossed with radical feminist ideas that see women as having a special and even mystical relationship to nature, through the traditions of herbal healing and witchcraft, through women's more intimate relationship with the reproduction of human life, through the magical correlation of the menstrual cycle with the phases of the moon, and so on. Lesbianism here is not an object choice but the means to achieve full recognition of this repressed or despised femininity without the repressive, destructive presence of masculinity and male sexuality. Such lesbian imagery is just as involved, on the one hand, with typifica-tion in its depiction of a range of variations on a clearly recognizable type, and on the other with a conventional view of nature. To say so, however, is to speak from within the very denaturalizing, rationalistic perspective that such imagery, with good reason, opposes.

Figure 4.23 Lesbian feminist typification: JEB, 'Jane. Willits, California. 1977', from *Eye to Eye: Portraits of Lesbians*, Washington, DC (1979)

Figure 4.24 Lesbian feminist typification: JEB, 'Joan. Mt. Rainier, Maryland. 1979', from *Eye to Eye: Portraits of Lesbians*, Washington, DC (1979)

Figure 4.25 Lesbian feminist typification: JEB, 'Flo. Flint Hill, Virginia. 1978', from *Eye to Eye: Portraits of Lesbians*, Washington, DC (1979)

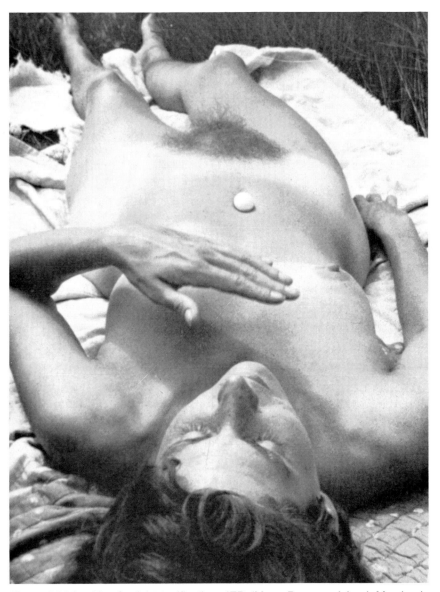

Figure 4.26 Lesbian feminist typification: JEB, 'Mara. Broomes Island, Maryland. 1976', from *Eye to Eye: Portraits of Lesbians*, Washington, DC (1979). 'Under the domination of the egg, one usually finds a prevalence of peaceful, uterine life, satiated, comfortable, complacent, though determined in its defense against outsiders. A matriarchal realm hardly knows such a thing as a war of conquest, although the defense of the domestic egg is stalwart and brave' (Helen Diner, *Mother and Amazons: The First Feminine History of Culture*, New York: Julian Press, 1965)

SUMMARY

My purpose in this article has been to explore some of the complexity behind the apparently simple face of gay types. This very complexity gives them their force, for good or ill, as a mode of representation. The complexity springs in part from the nature of typification, which always condenses a wealth of social knowledge into a few striking and vivid signs. It springs in turn from the types' connectedness to other enormously complex sign systems, for example, competing conceptions of nature and mythologies such as Christianity or the vampire tale. Above all, it springs from the creativity of gay people in producing such rich and varied cultural systems, endowing such simple images with a range of contradictory meanings.

Studies in Visual Communication 9 (2) (spring 1983)

NOTE

1 This type is discussed and illustrated further in Chapter 6 below.

REFERENCES

Fischer, Hal (1978) *Gay Semiotics: A Photographic Study of Visual Coding among Homosexual Men*, Berkeley: NFS Press.

Gagnon, John and Simon, William (1973) *Sexual Conduct: The Sources of Human Sexuality*, Chicago: Aldine.

JEB (1979) *Eye to Eye: Portraits of Lesbians*, Washington DC: Glad Hag Books.

Perkins, T. E. (1979) 'Rethinking Stereotypes', in Michèle Barrett, Philip Corrigan, Annette Kuhn and Janet Wolff (eds) *Ideology and Cultural Production*, London: Croom Helm, 135–59.

FURTHER READING

Boffin, Tessa and Fraser, Jean (eds) (1991) *Stolen Glances: Lesbians Take Photographs*, London: Pandora.

Butler, Judith (1990) *Gender Trouble*, New York: Routledge.

Chesebro, James W. (ed.) (1981) *Gayspeak: Gay Male and Lesbian Communication*, New York: Pilgrim Press.

Fuss, Diana (ed.) (1991) *Inside/Out*, New York: Routledge.

Grahn, Judy (1984) *Another Mother Tongue: Gay Words, Gay Worlds*, Boston: Beacon.

Hetze, Stefanie (1986) *Happy-End für wen? Kino und lesbische Frauen*, Frankfurt-am-Main: tende.

Pearce, Frank (1973) 'How to be Immoral and Ill, Pathetic and Dangerous, All at the Same Time: Mass Media and Homosexuality', in Stanley Cohen and Jack Young (eds) *The Manufacture of News*, London: Constable, 284–301.

Russo, Vito (1981) *The Celluloid Closet*, New York: Harper & Row.

Weiss, Andrea (1992) *Vampires and Violets: Lesbians in the Cinema*, London:

Jonathan Cape.
Zimmerman, Bonnie (1981) 'Lesbian Vampires', *Jump Cut* 24/5: 23–4.
Zita, Jacqueline (1981) 'Counter Currencies of a Lesbian Iconography', *Jump Cut* 24/5: 26–30.

Chapter 5

Homosexuality and film noir

Some of the first widely available images of homosexuality in our time were those provided by the American film noir. Given the dearth of alternative images, it is reasonable to suppose that these had an important influence on both public ideas about homosexuality and, damagingly, gay self-images. I know that as I grew up realizing I was gay I used to identify with characters like Waldo in *Laura* or Jo in *A Walk on the Wild Side*; they concretized and reinforced for me the negative feelings about myself that I'd picked up elsewhere in the culture. I know from work within the gay movement how widespread these images still are among gays and non-gays alike. It is important then to understand these images as one aspect of the armoury of gay oppression and indeed of sexual oppression generally. How gays are represented is always part and parcel of the sexual ideology[1] of a culture and, as I hope my examination of film noir shows, also indicates the complex, ambiguous ways in which heterosexual women and men are thought and felt about in that culture.

These images are found way beyond the film noir proper, in the thriller in general and in the representation of gays in all kinds of films. The *Killing of Sister George*, for instance, in the theatre a comedy, became heavily noir in the film version, especially in the final seduction scene. Even films trying to be liberal towards gays, such as *Advise and Consent* or *The Detective*, when searching for a mode of representing gays and the gay lifestyle end up by drawing largely on the mode set by film noir.

To understand what these images mean, we have to look at their formation within the film noir, which constitutes their most determinant context. Although much of the imagery can be traced back to elements outside film noir in literature and certain reaches of the gay sub-culture, it acquired its crucial meaning from the way it was inflected in the film noir: the role of the gays in the films' plot structures, their association with aspects of the films' 'world', their characteristically noir filmic treatment. The form this article takes then is first an attempt to define and delineate the film noir, followed by a discussion of the role of gayness within it.

WHAT IS FILM NOIR?

There is quite a lot of disagreement about film noir, both over what kind of phenomenon it is (a genre? a mood? a style? a cycle?) and over what films are to be included in it. Paul Schrader's desire in his useful article (1972) to term it a 'mood' is understandable, thereby emphasizing its affective quality and acknowledging how much 'looser' it is as a film kind than the Western, the gangster thriller or the backstage musical. Yet if its characteristic mood or feel is what is most important about it, this is none the less a highly specific quality and not just some generalized pessimism or Angst which one can find in an enormous range of films. Moreover, a mood is not something that is poured over a film or injected into it but is carried by identifiable aesthetic features. It seems to me that there are such features at the levels of *structure*, *iconography* and *visual style* that recur from film noir to film noir and thereby identify it as a discrete film kind, and that just such an observable continuity in a batch of films is what makes that batch a genre.

What does make film noir different from most other film genres is its history. As a continuous run of films, it lasted only from 1941 (*The Maltese Falcon*) to 1955 (*Kiss Me Deadly*). Elements of its generic features can of course be traced back to earlier films or film types (e.g., Warner Brothers' gangster films, German expressionism, French poetic realism, etc.), but it is the specific conjunction of all the aesthetic features that characterizes the genre as a genre. After 1955 there have been films that have worked within the noir conventions – stragglers like *A Walk on the Wild Side* (1962), reworkings like *P. J.* (1967) (British title: *A New Face in Hell*) and *Gunn* (1967), self-conscious nostalgia/parody films like *Chinatown* (1974), *The Long Goodbye* (1973) and *Farewell My Lovely* (1976). I have included the later films in my discussion of the role of gayness in film noir, partly because they make explicit what had to be implicit or marginal in the earlier films. However, in this section I have restricted discussion to the main period, since exactly what counts from later periods is controversial.

Let me now suggest the generic aesthetic features of film noir in terms of structure, iconography and visual style.

Structure

The basic structure of film noir is like a labyrinth with the hero as the thread running through it. He starts out on a quest to solve a mystery (Spade, Marlowe, Dana Andrews in *Laura* (1944), Bogart in *Dead Reckoning*) or else to find work (*Detour*), settle down (*Kiss of Death*), commit murder (*The Postman Always Rings Twice*, *Double Indemnity*), become a great boxer (*Body and Soul*). Yet the road that he chooses, or is chosen for him, does not lead directly.

Think of the standard detective story of Conan Doyle or Agatha Christie in which every incident contributes to the hero detective's understanding of the crime and is used in the final scene to demonstrate the guilty party. This is quite different from film noir. Here, whole episodes which seem to be furthering the quest turn out to have been a waste of time and energy. For instance, in *Strangers on a Train* (1951), Guy is going to tell Bruno's father what a psychopathic son he's got, down corridors, up stairs, past dog, dead of night – only to find himself talking to Bruno. Or, in *Farewell My Lovely* (1945), what appears to be an unconnected path (Moose's search for Wanda) turns out to be a key to the mystery, while Spade's visit to Jules Amthor, where he is drugged, has to fight his way through cobwebs in front of his eyes and then through the doors and corridors of the house, tells him very little (and takes up a lot of screen time). The detour may in fact take him away from the quest altogether, most notably in *Detour* (1945), where Al is so far deflected from his trek across America in search of work that he never gets back to it. And of course sometimes the whole film can be seen to have been a pointless quest, as is the case with *The Maltese Falcon*.

The labyrinth can come out as repetition with the hero going over the same ground several times. For instance, in *Fear in the Night* (1947), the murder is repeated as waking dream, uncanny recall and under fake (or is it?) hypnosis; or *Postman* (1945), which is entirely structured around a series of repetitions (two attempts to run away, two attempts to kill Nick, two trials for murder, the echo by the lake, the title) as well as being characterized by characters' endlessly returning to the same place (no matter how often they leave the place, Cora and Frank are forced to come back to the café).

The labyrinth is sometimes reflected in the geography of individual incidents – as in *Niagara* (1953), with the complex of walkways and stairs at the foot of the falls, and later around the clock tower as Monroe tries to flee Cotton; the mirror mazes in *Fear in the Night* and *The Lady from Shanghai* (1947); or the nightclub in *Gilda* (1946), where mirrors turn out to be doors, and walls turn out to be windows.

The menace of the labyrinth is often heightened by the film's failure to fulfil two of the dominant expectations we have of film stories – that mysteries will be solved and that the heterosexual couple will get together. It is not that mysteries go entirely unsolved, but the presentation often makes it feel as if they do. The detective's explanation *à la* Holmes or Poirot is often so breathless as to be incomprehensible, as in *Farewell My Lovely* and *The Big Sleep*. Ambiguity often lingers over the complicity of a central figure, as with Dix in *In a Lonely Place* (1950) and the many femmes fatales of the form. In the case of *Kiss Me Deadly* (1955), we don't really know what the explosion is that Hammer's opening the box unleashes. Is it a bomb? It's not really big enough for the A-bomb. Hammer's involvement with the box comes through women. Is it perhaps mythically, misogynistically, Pandora's box? That would perhaps be a satisfactory metaphorical end to the film but hardly a material solution to the mystery.

The settling down of the heterosexual couple is often denied us. Spade sends Brigit to the chair in *The Maltese Falcon* (1941); Laurel refuses Dix even though she knows he's technically innocent in *In a Lonely Place*; Phyllis and Walter shoot each other in *Double Indemnity* (1944). The separation or destruction of a couple early on in the film may be final, as in *The Big Heat* and *Detour*. Alternatively, the heterosexual resolution often appears to be the required ending tacked on to couplings that would seem recipes for marital disaster, especially those between Johnny and Gilda, McPherson and Laura.

Further noir feeling is induced by the use of flash-back, voice-over and dream structures. These may have two effects. Firstly, they may cast into doubt the status-as-truth of the events presented. Much of the power of the cinema resides in the belief in seeing-as-believing. Although easily exposed as fraudulent theoretically, the realism/naturalism of the cinema is best not ignored as an -ism, holding considerable sway over how we see films in the ordinary way of things. Because of it, the flash-back was generally treated until film noir as simply the truth, no matter how introduced (as memory, confession, verbal explanation, etc.) When in the trial scene in the modern story in *Intolerance* (1915), Robert Harron tells the court that he gave the murder weapon back to the gang boss before the murder was committed, this is presented as a very brief flash-back. Here there is no question of treating this testimony as evidence in the way a jury should, sifting it for lies or the distortions of memory. Rather the film assures us that this *is* what happened. However, with film noir, where flash-back is often extensively used, uncertainties begin to creep in. There are discontinuities between overlapping versions shown in flash-back of what happened in *Crossfire* (1947); dreams are presented with the logic of reality in *The Woman in the Window* (1944), or turn out to have been reality (*Fear in the Night*), while realities are presented with the strangeness (Gloria Grahame and ménage in *Crossfire*) or the erotic intensity (*Out of the Past*, 1947) of a dream. Moreover, the highly emotional context of the telling may cast doubt on the reliability of the version of the story told. Thus we have a confession during a thunderstorm in *Dead Reckoning* (1947), or a wounded man careering through streets in a car and then pouring it all out into a recorder in *Double Indemnity*. There is by no means a wholesale reversal of the standard earlier flash-back convention in film noir, but it does mark a partial departure from it which, in the context of the certainty over pictorial truthfulness prevalent in Hollywood, feels disconcerting.

Flash-backs, voices-over and dream structures may be the means of suggesting that the progress through the labyrinth is the working out of a fated or fatal pattern. The end is known to the voice-over from the beginning even if not always to us, and all the events can be seen as leading inevitably, inexorably and gratuitously to it. The voice-over may spell this out, as in *Detour* (1945), or it may simply imply it by picking on the significant moments that pointed downhill (*Postman*). The nature of fate is sometimes explicitly examined in film noir, usually in the form of a character with uncontrollable ('Freudian') impulses within him/her, as in *In a Lonely Place*, *Lady of Deceit*, *The Stranger on the Third Floor* (1941) and *On Dangerous Ground* (1951). But these are films without flash-backs or voices-over, and they make fatality to a degree comprehensible even if leaving it frighteningly uncontrollable. The flash-back, on the other hand, is both vaguer as to the nature of destiny and fate and more frightening. It gives the aesthetic structure of predestination without any ontological back-up to make it comprehensible.

Iconography

The concept 'iconography' drawn from the work of art historian Erwin Panofsky (1955), has proved particularly generative for work on film genre, as for instance in Ed Buscombe's 'The Idea of Genre' (on the Western) (1970) and Colin McArthur's *Underworld USA* (1972). It may be defined as the study of the set of images (objects, people, settings), sounds and music shared by a run of films that marks them off as a genre. Icons are the cues that immediately indicate to us, 'This is a Western/science fiction/ kung fu/ . . . film'. In the case of the Western or the gangster film, this set is very tight, precise and restricted, but there is nothing like that for film noir. However, if we use iconography in a slightly broader sense to refer to *types* of setting and star, there are some characteristic features.

Settings

These are at the two extremes of the city and the rural desert. In the former, film noir takes over many of the meanings associated with city iconography in the gangster film, as evoked by Robert Warshow (1964) and Colin McArthur (1972): desolation, brutality, threat and alienation, as caught in images of pavements glistening with rain, ill-lit streets, dingy bars and grubby rooming-houses. An important noir inflection of this set of images is the increased importance of the luxurious mansions and nightclubs. In the gangster film, these symbolize the pinnacle of the protagonist's rise to temporary power, but in film noir, they become the permanent environment of the hero's employers (not only those of the private eyes but also of employers in, for instance, *Gilda*, *Out of the Past* and *Sunset Boulevard* (1950)). The identification of luxury and a certain sort of good taste (seen in baroque art, exotic plants) with decadence and evil is central to film noir.

As for films noirs set in the country, the country is as desolate in its way as the city landscapes. Long deserted dusty roads are the countryside of *Postman* and *Detour*, and the Western *Pursued* (1947), generally regarded as part film noir, uses the barest and most fruitless Western scenery imaginable.

Settings tend to be in the public world rather than domestic. For the hero a basic domestic ritual like eating is transferred from family to public eating place. Indeed, the lunch counter comes close to being one of the true icons of the form (as in *Postman*, *The Killers* (1946), *The Stranger on the Third Floor* and *Out of the Past*). Crucial personal encounters take place not in the home but, say, in a train (*Strangers on a Train*), in a supermarket (*Double Indemnity*) or in a seedy cafe (Mexican sequence of *Out of the Past*).

In this way the hero is denied an environment of safety, cosiness or rootedness. If such an atmosphere is evoked at all, it serves to sharpen the depiction of the noir world by being under threat from the latter (*Kiss of Death*) or actually destroyed by it (*The Big Heat*). There is some play on this in *In a Lonely Place*, with its telling images of the unmade bed before Laurel moves in, her bringing Dix coffee, and the scene in the kitchen where he attacks the grapefruit with the serrated knife that he has through ignorance straightened out, thus linking lack of domesticity and violent impulse. More usually, when homes are shown, they are the homes of the villains and moreover are 'abnormal' – they belong to single (i.e., 'incomplete') people as in *Laura*, or childless couples as in *Gilda* or *Postman*, or of course, gays as in *Rope* (1948). That these homes are abnormal is iconographically expressed once again in a style of luxury quite different from the cosy normality of the 'ordinary family home'.

Stars

It is not so much specific stars (though there are Bogart, Mitchum, Lake, Graham) as certain types of star which characterize film noir.

The appearance of women in film noir has been felicitously described by Colin McArthur as being of 'startlingly unreal sensuality' (figure 5.1). It is above all in the faces that this quality is produced. Makeup and coiffure are used in a way that draws attention to their own artifice while at the same time they create surfaces of considerable tactile impact and draw attention to aspects of the head such as the mouth and hair which are particularly associated with eroticism in our time. The long faces of Lauren Bacall, Veronica Lake and Lizbeth Scott are emphasized by waves of hair hanging down around them; the hair is groomed and lit lustrously, it flows in 'natural curves' that have yet somehow obviously been coiffed; the foundation makeup makes the face very pale while the lips are heavy and dark. To this combination of artifice and sensuality is frequently added the use of luxurious clothes made of highly tactile, yet man-made fibres, and of course furs are often used to identify women with savage nature.

For the heroes it is the imagery of hard-boiledness that prevails, with unpressed suits, ties loosened at the neck, low drawn hats and unshaven faces (figure 5.2). This bespeaks the heroes' lack of concern about their

Figure 5.1 Veronica Lake: startlingly unreal sensuality

appearance and also indicates, social conventions being what they are, that these men are not married.

Visual style

To discuss the influence of German expressionism on film noir (chiaroscuro lighting, unbalanced composition, skewed camera angles) is a standard

Figure 5.2 Hard-boiled looks: Dick Powell in *Murder My Sweet* (USA 1945)

part of film noir analysis, most notably in an article by J. A. Place and L. S. Peterson (1974). Although the full extent of the expressionist visual repertoire is only discernible in a minority of films (*Stranger on the Third Floor, The Killers, Farewell my Lovely*), in a modified version use of shadow and unbalanced composition does characterize film noir. For a fuller exploration of this, see the Place and Peterson article.

GAYS IN FILM NOIR

How are gays represented in film noir, and what are they doing in it? To see the iconography of gayness in film noir, let me straight away list some relevant characters and the iconographic features that label them gay:

Film	Characters	Traits
Female characters		
In a Lonely Place	Martha (figure 5.3)	Big-boned, hair drawn back, aggressive, hard voice
Rebecca (1940)	Mrs Danvers	Severe, hair drawn back, hard voice
A Walk on the Wild Side (1962)	Jo (figure 5.4)	Tailored suits, shortish hair, overall military precision of dress
Tony Rome (1967)	Irene	Fat, shortish hair, loud voiced
Farewell My Lovely (1976)	Frances Amthor (figure 5.5)	Fat, shortish hair, loud voiced
Male characters		
The Maltese Falcon	Cairo (figure 5.6)	Fastidious dress, crimped hair, perfume
Strangers on a Train	Bruno	Fastidious dress, manicured nails
Laura	Waldo (figure 5.8)	Fastidious dress, love of art, bitchy wit
Farewell My Lovely (1944)	Lindsay	Fastidious dress, knowledge of clothes, jewellery, perfume
Farewell My Lovely (1976)	Lindsay	(same)
Brute Force	Captain Munsey	Fastidious dress, love of art, music
The Big Sleep	General Sternwood	Hothouse atmosphere (this is most tenuous example)
P. J.	Quel	Gaudy clothes, fussy hairstyle
Rope	Brandon, Philip (figure 5.7)	Fastidious dress, love of art, music, cuisine

Several initial points may be made about the list above. Firstly, it is clearly only in a minority of films noirs that gay characters appear (I doubt if I have missed more than two or three), yet their absence from all other types of film and the caution with which even film noir had to introduce them suggests that they do none the less constitute a defining feature of film noir taken as a whole. Secondly, it will be noted how the iconography of male and female gays contrasts with that of straight men and women in film noir, not to the extent of cross-dressing but in terms of glamorous and sensual as opposed to rough and severe for women, and carelessness as opposed to fastidiousness for men. Thirdly, the iconography was not of course developed for film noir alone but

Figure 5.3 Butch dyke (Ruth Gillette) confronts hard-boiled hero (Humphrey Bogart) in *In a Lonely Place* (USA 1950)

has its roots in gay literature and lifestyles (here distorted and denigrated). It is noticeable that the lesbian iconography is less elaborated and precise than that for gay men (because lesbian culture has had greater difficulty in developing under the double oppression of gayness and femaleness). Fourthly, what is significant about the iconography is that it is not explicitly sexual. Gays are thus defined by everything but the very thing that makes us different.

What are these gay characters doing in film noir? In the first instance, they are a further amplification of images of sexual decadence and perversion prevalent in the form:

Nymphomania	*The Big Sleep*
Pornography	*The Big Sleep*
Old man + young woman	*Farewell My Lovely, Postman, Gilda, Niagara, Woman in The Window, P. J.*
Old woman + young man	*Laura, Sunset Boulevard, P. J.*
Sado-masochism	*Pursued, The Big Heat, Brute Force, Rope of Sand* (1949), *Strangers on a Train, Kiss me Deadly, Rope*
Incest	*Pursued*
Transvestism	*Gunn* (I have not included this character as gay as there is no indication that he is, in fact, homosexual)

Figure 5.4 Smart butch Jo (Barbara Stanwyck) in *A Walk on the Wild Side* (USA 1962)

This in turn relates to the central image of sexuality in the films – the femme fatale.

These images are all related first iconographically. Nearly all form part of the luxury milieu. Waldo in *Laura* is the epitome of this (figure 5.8). The opening tracking shot of the film round a room full of neatly arranged,

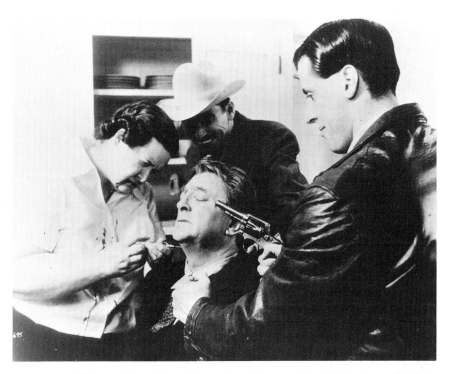

Figure 5.5 Vicious dyke (Kate Murtagh) puts hypodermic into hero (Robert Mitchum) in *Farewell My Lovely* (USA 1976)

over-fussy objets d'art immediately places the milieu, and his subsequently revealed obsession with clothes, wines, gossip and the arts confirms it. His witty heartlessness is first rammed home in his line, 'I should be sincerely sorry to see my neighbours' children devoured by wolves', a line which calls attention to his childlessness and hence sexual 'unnaturalness'. Similarly we see or judge Quel (overdressed in shiny Kaftan tops) as housekeeper to Orbison's mistress, the nightclub in *Gilda*, the hothouse opening of *The Big Sleep*, the penthouse apartment in *Rope*.

The association of gayness and the luxury milieu works differently for the lesbian characters. In most cases, they are shown as *working* in this setting, as housekeeper (Mrs Danvers), masseuse (Martha), or owner–manager (Jo, Frances). This means that the milieu less clearly defines their character. It is determined by their employers in the first two cases, while Jo and Frances as brothel keepers are supplying an ambience defined by the wants of men. This emphasis on lesbians as working women always carries strong elements of tyranny and violence, of servants towards mistresses (Mrs Danvers, Martha), of madames to their girls. This tyranny then shades into the characters' feelings of attraction to the woman in question.

Figure 5.6 Fastidious queen (Peter Lorre) and immaculate femme fatale (Mary Astor) in *The Maltese Falcon* (USA 1941)

The equation of lesbian love with tyranny is also the strongest impression we get from the scene between Irene and Georgia in the caravan in *Tony Rome* and between George and Childie in *The Killing of Sister George* (1969). The tyrannic *form* of employer/employee relationships which is established by the place of the lesbian relationship in the world of the

Figure 5.7 Fastidious and immaculate young men (Farley Granger (right) and John Dall) with mentor (James Stewart) in *Rope* (USA 1948)

classic film noir thus carries over into films where the lesbian characters are supposed to be each other's social equal.

The gay men and the femmes fatales share the same decor iconographically. The reason for this is spelled out in *Laura*. Women can legitimately be identified with luxury, with obsessions with beauty and appearance – Laura herself is the epitome of all that is alluring in such a world. Men who are associated with it, however, be they gay (Waldo) or gigolos (Shelby), are weak, villainous or depraved (or all three). Hence, the touchstone of male normality in *Laura*, McPherson (Dana Andrews), is very much an outsider to the milieu and largely repelled by it except in so far as he is attracted to its feminine representative, Laura. The ideological pairing of male homosexuality with luxury and decadence (with connotations of impotence and sterility) is of a piece with the commonplace linking of women with luxury (women as expensive things to win and keep, women as bearers of their husbands' wealth) and decadence (women as beings without sexuality save for the presence of men). The feeling that gay men are *like* women yet *not* women produces the 'perverse' tone of this mode of iconographic representation.

Figure 5.8 Elegant queen (Clifton Webb) and luxury milieu in *Laura* (USA 1944)

In terms of narrative structure the gay characters, when not actually villains (Cairo, Bruno, Waldo), frequently constitute one of the blind alleys of the labyrinth, lengthening the process of solving the mystery or threatening the heterosexual union. Examples of the former process are *Tony Rome* (Rome learns nothing from tracking down and cross-examining Georgia and Irene) and *Farewell My Lovely* (1945 – all Lindsay does is lead Marlowe to being a murder suspect; 1976 – sequence in Jules Amthor's house (see above) becomes the sequence in Frances Amthor's brothel). In *P. J.* Quel is there specifically to send P. J. in one direction while he thinks he's going in the other, and the visit to the seedy 'Gay Caballero' in search of promised information yields P. J. nothing but a beating. Examples of threatening a heterosexual union occur in *In a Lonely Place* (Martha sows seeds of doubt in Laurel's mind; and the placing of the scene in which she appears, between the scene in the nightclub where Laurel and Dix feel they are under surveillance and the scene in which Sylvia blurts out that Laurel has seen the police again without telling Dix, seems to suggest Martha is a link in the chain of the couple's gradual separation), *Walk on the Wild Side* (Jo keeps Hally and Dove apart), *Laura* (where Waldo always acts to keep McPherson and Laura, and indeed Laura and all her men, apart and ultimately emerges as the villain) and *Strangers on a Train* (where ironically Bruno's murdering Miriam to make Guy free to marry Anne actually makes it more difficult for them to marry because of the suspicion of murder hanging over Guy). In the case of the last mentioned film, there is a particularly close fit between the labyrinth structure and homosexuality. Guy's visit to Bruno's parents' house accomplishes neither its overt purpose (the murder) nor its covert purpose (warning Bruno's father). But since Bruno has set this up and since Guy finds himself talking to Bruno, who is waiting for Guy in bed in his pyjamas, may we not, as Gerald Peary has suggested to me, read this as a blind alley actually constructed in the hope of homosexual seduction?

In most instances, gays function as both villains and frustrations of the heterosexual development, as do the femmes fatales. This in fact seems to be central to film noir. One has only to compare the standard police film, in which family/sex life is always seen in opposition to or as a respite from the hero's job, to see how distinctive is film noir's intertwining of the job (nailing the villain) and sex (getting it together with the woman).

Our society distinguishes with some anxiety the public world of work from the private world of family, affection and sexuality, on the assumption that the instrumental purposes of work (getting things done, making money, acting efficiently) would be undermined by too much emotional or sexual by-play. Film noir, however, tends to collapse these two worlds into each other. The hero's work becomes sexual: McPherson falls in love with the woman whose 'death' he is investigating; looking after Gilda becomes Johnny's job; a brothel (*A Walk on the Wild Side*) is actually a place of sexual labour; Joe in *Sunset Boulevard* is employed virtually as a stud. The women are involved in the plot not just as a 'love-interest' but as agents and enemies: Brigid uses her charms to trick Spade and to attempt to acquire the Falcon; Cora suffuses the café with sexuality in *Postman*. Similarly, gay men introduce a permanent sexual potential into the world of work. They are unsettling to the puritan (non-sexual) safety of the instrumental world. The work of intellectual discussion in *Rope* is undermined by the actual erotically charged realization at the start of the film of what they are supposedly only talking about. Quel appraises P. J.'s body before employing him, spies on him and Maureen dancing together, chats him up at the dance in Haiti, invites him to a gay club to give him information (actually to have him beaten up) – in other words, the films endlessly introduces a sexual current into what should be 'straightforward' moments of employment, surveillance and investigation. Lesbians provide a further turn of the screw – as women with *jobs* (not just *roles* as wives, mothers or lovers) they enter the instrumental world, but because they are women they can also act in concert with other women, thus effectively blocking the hero in both the instrumental and the sexual spheres. Examples are the closed encounter of Rome with Georgia and Irene, the sense of two women ganging up on a man in *In a Lonely Place* and *Rebecca*, and the triumph of Jo's world, the brothel, over Dove's love and career.

The sexuality of film noir is also distinctive in that it does not require an initiative on the part of the hero to activate it. The gays' sexuality is developed before the coming of the hero, while the femmes fatales are often notable for their taking the initiative in and expressing their sexuality (e.g., Cora, Gilda, Lauren Bacall in *The Big Sleep*). However, their sexual independence from the hero is undercut by the principle that no sexual satisfaction is possible away from the hero. The femme fatale (like the nymphomaniac) is an image of frustration, alive with sexual desire that cannot be satisfied. This is often expressed by her being attached to an older man or an indifferent gang boss. Such an image is amplified in the gay characters by the culturally widespread notion (reinforced by the non-sexuality of the gay iconography) that gays are intensely physical beings who cannot 'do anything' physically and hence vibrate with frustrated twisted sexual energy. This is most true of lesbian characters. The introduction of Martha as a masseuse handling Laurel's flesh is the most physical yet non-sexual (in the genital sense) image in the film. As Martha tells Laurel to leave Dix, the shot from below suggests the intense physicality and frustration of the being whose sexuality attempts to operate independently of the hero. Similarly we have the shot of Jo in *A Walk on the Wild Side* with her back to the camera and the squared-up shoulders of her perfectly tailored suit physically present against the light of the window. She is saying, 'Sometimes I've waited years for what I've wanted', while stretched languorously across the bed in a lace house-coat is what she really wants, Hally. (Later Jo is made to utter a supposedly gay credo setting its sights against eroticism: 'Can any man love a woman for herself, give her the beauty of life without the reek of lust?') Inflections of the images are also realized in male gay characters. Waldo expresses his eroticism in idealizing Laura, no more sleeping with or loving her than he does any of his other objets d'art; Lindsay in *Farewell My Lovely* is physically alive by virtue of an interest in perfumes and women's clothes; Munsey in *Brute Force* (and presumably Paul Henreid in *Rope of Flesh*) expresses his gayness through a sadistic beating.

Sexuality independent of the hero is shown to be neurotic, frustrated, and sour; yet it also means that the hero's own sexuality goes unchallenged. Approached by a 'faggot', or a femme fatale, the hero has the whole moral force of Hollywood and western culture and male chauvinism to fall back on in order to refuse the offer. But in this way his own sexual adequacy is not tested. It is of course to be assumed – film noir does not call the potency of male sexuality into question. Yet there hovers around it an implication of male uncertainty about sexuality; and here the gay characters start to serve a different function from that of the femmes fatales.

Several films noirs feature soldiers who have just left, or are about to leave, the service (*Dead Reckoning*, *Crossfire*, *The Blue Dahlia* (1945)). These films were made at the period when men were returning from active service, sometimes several years after living with women. The all-male group often seems the norm in noir films, not only those just mentioned but also in *Brute Force*, *The Big Heat* (where Debbie is excluded from the gambling scene) and the men's club of *The Woman in the Window*. The intense relationship of two men is also common as in *Dead Reckoning* (Bogart: 'He was laughing, tough and lonesome'; to Scott: 'I loved him more than you'), *The Big Combo* (1955) (Bettini cries when Fante is killed by dynamite 'Don't leave me, Fante!', and turns stool pigeon), *Double Indemnity* (Walter and Keyes). Of course, this is not confined to film noir. It is true of Westerns, Howard Hawks, or even, according to Leslie Fiedler (1960), the whole of American literature. But perhaps the potential homosexuality of all-male groups and male–male relationships is much nearer the surface in both the image of armed service and prison life and the experience of it too. In this context the gay characters serve as an example of sick male–male relationships (that is, sexual ones) over against healthy (non-sexual) ones. Lest we imagine Gallagher 'loves' Joe in *Brute Force*, we have Munsey to remind us what a perverted male–male relationship is like. Lest we imagine Spade's suspicion of Brigit is itself suspicious, we have Cairo and Guttman to remind us of how far Spade is removed from that sort of thing.

Gilda has a different emphasis. Here the hero (Glenn Ford/Johnny) does have a close relationship with another man (Charles Farrel/Ballen) which is implicitly homosexual, and this does cast doubts on his reaction to the femme fatale (Rita Hayworth/Gilda) and indeed upon the actual 'fatal' quality of the latter. The gayness of the Johnny–Ballen relationship is implicitly yet definitely enough etched in, even without use of the gay iconography. There is dialogue about the three of us (Johnny, Ballen and Ballen's cane) who will never be split up by anything or anyone; exchanged glances are held longer than glances between non-sexual partners normally are; Ballen 'picks up' Johnny for no apparent reason (altruism is not presented as one of his characteristics), and Johnny has no observable talent apart from being pretty; and perhaps I may be forgiven for quoting one of the first lines in the film (dubious evidence here), where Johnny says to Ballen, 'You must lead a gay life'. Later, even Gilda emphasizes the parallels between herself and Johnny as Ballen's pick-ups.[2]

When Gilda turns up as Ballen's wife, Johnny's reaction can be read as straight jealousy. But the film also provides another reason, which in turn provides a (naive) explanation for his relationship with Ballen – namely, they are an old affair that somehow went sour. This is why he resents Gilda, but it might also be 'why' he is in a gay relationship, that she has put him off women.

Two points amplify this interpretation. First of all, we have to be careful not to assess the characterization of Gilda by today's standards – perhaps in 1946 her really quite mild promiscuity was shocking. The advertising for *Gilda* played her up as a bad woman, and Hayworth had made a notable appearance as a femme fatale in *Blood and Sand* (1941). Yet her image outside of *Gilda* is also close to that developed later by Monroe – innocent sexuality or woman as the Life Force. Certainly it is something like this that she embodies in the musicals and her dancing (with its Latin-ness that is carefree but not vulgarly sensual) and perhaps in *Only Angels Have Wings* (1939). There seems to be at least as much carry-over of this innocent sexuality as of the femme fatale of film noir in the first shot of her, which in a close-up catches her on a movement, head-up, throwing back her hair from across her face, looking and smiling straight past the camera. Then again, she is given the song 'Put the Blame on Mame' to sing quietly in the deserted nightclub to the sympathetic and philosophical men's room attendant. Her friendship with a man who repeatedly stresses his distance from and contempt for the luxury milieu of the nightclub, the quiet reflectiveness of the setting and her delivery of the song (as she accompanies herself on a guitar), and of course the words of the song which point to the way men always put the blame on women's sexuality for natural disasters, all these imply that Gilda is far from fatal and that there is something 'pathological' in Johnny's soon violent response to her. (However, as the song suggests, his 'pathology' may be typical.)

The second amplification of this interpretation occurs after the apparent death of Ballen in the exploding aeroplane. Johnny and Gilda marry, but it is clear that the marriage is not consummated. The labyrinthine structures of the film, that have hitherto concentrated on Ballen, the mirror-maze effects of the nightclub and the impenetrability of his secret (tungsten), now shift to the Gilda character, who keeps leaving Johnny only to find herself brought back forcibly by him or one of his henchmen – notably in the sequence where she actually gets away to another country, picks up with another man ('a lawyer') and returns with him to Buenos Aires only to discover he was in the service of Johnny all along. The culmination of this is the famous striptease number, done to a defiantly sung 'Put the Blame on Mame'. Johnny watches. It is often said that this strip goes no further than a very suggestive removing of a pair of gloves, but although we don't see more than that, Gilda is in fact offering the fastenings in her dress to undo when Johnny drags her away and slaps her face. This is the first time we have seen any emotion or lack of control in Johnny, and it has been provoked only by an extreme sexual come-on from Gilda. After this, the marriage works. It is as if Johnny's 'normal' sexuality can only be aroused through a violent confrontation with a woman. Concepts of the inherent sado-masochism of heterosexual relationships hover around this sense of violence and have already been hinted at in the image of Gilda with a whip at the Mardi Gras ball and in the character of Ballen, with his phallic knife-cane, his thin-lipped, scarred face, and his references to the excitement of cruelty and 'other strong emotions'. What *Gilda* seems to point to is something that most films noirs try to keep at bay – that all sexuality or all male sexuality is sick. Where most films noirs evoke sick sexuality every-where except in the hero, *Gilda* has him caught between gayness, in no way presented positively, and sado-masochism.

Of the films noirs I have seen, in *Gilda* alone is the adequacy of male sexuality questioned.[3] It is perhaps implicit in others: with McPherson's obsession with the 'dead' Laura, for instance, or the dark sadistic side of Dix in *In a Lonely Place* (though the sexuality of this is not explored). But usually male sexual adequacy is ensured because the hero's adequacy is taken as read but not demonstrated. Heroes just are sexually adequate unless we are told to the contrary. And to deflect any doubts that linger, we have such unambiguously sick images of frustration and maliciousness as the femmes fatales, nymphos, queers and dykes.

Jump Cut 16 (1977)

NOTES

1 There is not one simple sexual ideology in a culture. There is struggle between different ideologies, rooted in different material circumstances (male–female, straight–gay, etc.). There is contradiction between these ideologies and within them.

Chapter 6

Coming out as going in: the image of the homosexual as a sad young man

> No-one he knew was beset with the melancholia, emotional frigidity, or feminine symbolisms he found in himself.
>
> (*Maybe – Tomorrow*)

When I was growing up in the 1950s and 1960s, I assented that the lot of queers like myself was a melancholy one. I don't remember now exactly where I first picked up this idea, but I do remember recognizing my mood in lines like the above, or seeing myself in the characters of Geoff in *A Taste of Honey* and both Reggie and Pete in *The Leather Boys*, or knowing that books with covers showing pairs of young men looking mournfully downwards yet towards each other were for me.

I related to this stereotype of gay men as sad young men selectively. Like them I loved cookery, clothes and the arts and chose to ignore their taste for sewing and interior decoration, which I didn't share at all; like them, I had a penchant for dark-eyed, well-built chaps and just took no notice of their incomprehensible passion for the school football hero. I had different sorts of feeling about them too. I thought I virtually was Geoff in *A Taste of Honey* and David in *Giovanni's Room* (even though I was neither working class nor American), but it was more longing I felt towards Gaylord Le Claire in *Maybe – Tomorrow*, a wish that I could both be him and have him with his 'earnest face and handsome physique'. And I took on board the two main messages of the type – that to be homosexual was both irremediably sad and overwhelmingly desirable.

I don't claim that my relation to this stereotype is that of all other gay men of my generation, but I start with it, partly because I want to use myself in evidence of the fact that stereotypes can be both a complex and a formative mode of representation. We are accustomed to thinking of them as simple, repetitive, boring and prejudiced group images which, should they supposely be about ourselves, we angrily reject. We mistake their simplicity of formal means (a few broadly drawn, instantly identifiable signs endlessly repeated) and evident ideological purpose (to keep/put out-groups in their place) for a simplicity of connotation and actual ideological effect. What interests me in looking here at the gay man as sad young man is the way a stereotype can be complex, varied, intense and contradictory, an image of otherness in which it is still possible to find oneself.

> On a stage, empty but for some impressionistic, Noguchi-like set pieces, a young man . . . stabs the air with his arms in what seems like a futile attempt to break free from his past, and then doubles up in a foetal position while a flock of black-draped furies hover near. [. . .] He wants to go back to the days when he kissed a little girl among the hollyhocks, but this innocence is irretrievable and he turns to a young man for comfort. For this, the boy is taunted and gang-raped by a pack of schoolchums. With insult heaped upon injury, the boy kills himself . . .
>
> (*Monument for a Dead Boy*)[1]

The stereotype of the sad young man is found in probably all representational media, from novels and 'non-fiction' accounts (e.g. *Man on a*

Figure 6.1 Farley Granger

Figure 6.2 Dirk Bogarde

Pendulum, 'a case history of an invert presented by a religious counselor', told in a style broadly indistinguishable from novels like *The Divided Path* or *All the Sad Young Men*) to plays, films, even dance (e.g. *Monument for a Dead Boy*) and song ('Ballad of the Sad Young Men' recorded by Petula Clark and Roberta Flack). It is equally present in high and low culture, from critically acclaimed fiction (James Baldwin's *Giovanni's Room*) to soft-core pornography (Joe Leon Houston's *Desire in the Shadows* aka *The Gay Flesh*), and from avant-garde cinema (*Fragment of Seeking*, *Twice a Man*) via porn again (*Pink Narcissus*, *Passing Strangers*) to entertainment movies with 'serious themes' (*Rebel without a Cause*, *Tea and Sympathy*, *Victim*), though it seems to have remained doggedly middle-brow in the theatre (*The Green Bay Tree*, *The Immoralist*, *The Boys in the Band*). It is an important element in highly public star images such as Montgomery Clift, Sal Mineo, James Dean, Farley Granger (figure 6.1) and Dirk Bogarde (figure 6.2) just

Figure 6.3 Cedric Morris, *Self Portrait*, 1930 (Trustees of the National Portrait Gallery, London)

as in the more restrictedly circulated paintings of Christopher Wood or Cedric Morris (figure 6.3) (cf. Cooper 1986).

The examples I have taken throughout this discussion are all Anglo-American. There certainly are equivalents throughout northern European culture (and perhaps in southern), but this is not something I have explored further. Something of the stereotype's rhetoric is also evident in lesbian titles like *Women in the Shadows* and *We Walk Alone*, not to mention *The Well of Loneliness*, but the similarities and differences between such images of lesbians and the sad young man need exploring rather than assuming. The centrality of the stereotype is most marked in the 1940s, 1950s and 1960s, although examples can be found before and after this.

> The hero . . . is haunted by dream images of youths in muscular poses, dashes his worn-out mother's lovingly proffered breakfast-egg to the floor, and rushes

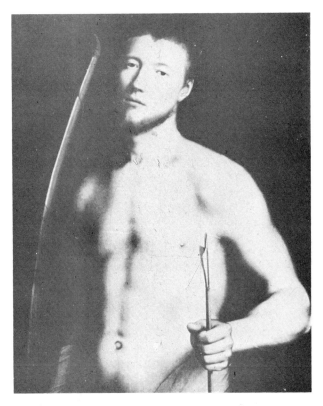

Figure 6.4 Antonio Moro, *Saint Sebastian*

out through grimy New York streets, until in the cemetery, he identifies his mother with the Virgin and his own suffering with Christ's, wallowing in the snow, between the graves, as if life were burial alive in some numb cold pain.
(*Images in the Snow*)[2]

Like all stereotypes, the sad young man is a combination and condensation of many traditions of representation. This intensifies the image (so much history of signification caught by such spare formal means), gives it rich possibilities of connotation and use and enables it to be read in a multiplicity of ways. The lineage of the sad young man includes:

Christianity, that is, the adoration of a naked, suffering young man, either Jesus or one of the martyrs, notably St Sebastian (figures 6.4 and 6.5), something discussed by de Becker as 'the latent homosexual structure of Christianity' (1967: 94) and by Castello as 'le plaisir de mourir';[3]

the Romantic poets, ostensibly biographically heterosexual, but feminized in their long-haired, ultra-pale looks and hyper-emotional personalities, thus representing correlations between physical appearance, emotional capacity and

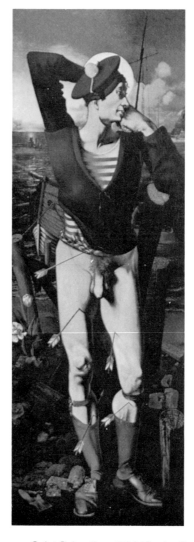

Figure 6.5 Alfred Courmes, *Saint Sebastian*, 1934 (Centre Georges Pompidou, Paris)

gender identity, while also yielding more imagery of the cadaverously beautiful young man, notably in Wallis's painting of the death of Chatterton (figure 6.6);

the Bildungsroman, and other traditions of the male coming of age novel, notably the Horatio Alger series, currently being re-read in terms of homo-eroticism (cf. Moon 1987);

the third sex (or 'congenital inversion'), the notion of a distinct bodily

Figure 6.6 Henry Wallis, *The Death of Chatterton*, 1856 (Trustees of the Tate Gallery, London)

type, the homosexual, placed on the cusp of male and female. Though only adhered to in the strictest biological sense by Magnus Hirschfeld, Havelock Ellis and others for a relatively short period,[4] versions of it (especially in terms of notions of a feminine personality within a male body) strongly persisted, often tricked out with

Freudianism, the popular perception of psychoanalytic ideas, including especially the notion of the dangers of narcissism and/or excessive closeness between mothers and boy children and the designation of homosexuality as a phase through which boys will pass (and in which they may get stuck). This in turn relates to

the invention of adolescence, the social construction of a distinct phase of individual development with its own attendant rituals and forms. Though there is disagreement about whether conceiving of such a phase is specific to western society, and if so when it emerged as a concept (Springhall 1983–4), its peculiar salience in twentieth-century western culture is widely attested, especially as the focus of both moral panics and, until the 1980s, of moral, especially sexual, progress;

urbanism as 'alienation', the tradition of perceiving the city as a world of loneliness, loosened moral order, fleeting, impermanent contact and love for sale.

> Theirs had been the laughter and the mocking pleasure – his the rounded shoulders, the sad eyes, the downturned mouth, the dismal apartment, the foggy windows . . .
>
> *(The Gay Year)*

The image of the sad young man is distilled on the covers of the books and novels centred on him (figures 6.7–6.17).

Most often, the people depicted are male. Women occasionally figure as on *Strange Brother* (figure 6.7) and *Tea and Sympathy* (figure 6.12). As in many of the narratives, she represents the sexual alternative to the sexuality troubling the sad young fellow. She offers herself sexually, in a pose which suggests at once the titillation of the sexually initiating woman, the lot of characters like Laura (*Tea and Sympathy*) of saving the boy by showing him he is capable of heterosexual sex and, most interestingly, the strong sense of the sad young man's desirability to heterosexual women, a theme often strongly marked in the books and presumably not irrelevant to the appeal of Clift *et al.*

The men on the covers are invariably white. There are examples of sad young black men as minor characters in the narratives, notably Johnny in *The L-Shaped Room*, yearning for the same straight boy as the heroine but with less success. However, I don't know of examples of main characters. Gay African-American writers have usually been distant or equivocal in their writings here, even James Baldwin making his sad young hero David in *Giovanni's Room* white. Though this may have been a self-protecting strategy on his part, it may also be because there is something specifically white about the stereotype. Black characters are often important in the narrative: Mark in *Strange Brother* is first discovered at a Harlem nightclub ('his face and hair stood out so extraordinarily fair, as he sat between two negro companions'); the white protagonists of both *All the Sad Young Men* and *Man on a Pendulum* have encounters with a young gay mulatto, the ultimate figure of in-between-ness, who is represented as happy with his lot in a manner that is not really possible for a white boy. In these examples, the sad young man's difference from black gay men is stressed and this perhaps has to do with the stereotype's roots in Christianity and the Romantic poets. The former, at the level of dominant representation of a white (and gentile) tradition, focuses on the suffering male body, the moral worth and erotic beauty of white male flesh always seen at the point of agony; the Romantic poet promotes the association of paleness with emotionality and femininity, from which it is but a short step to queer masculinity as white sensitivity. The sad young man becomes part of much wider constructions of white identity in terms of suffering (the burden which becomes the badge of our superiority).

Figure 6.7 *Strange Brother*, cover (1949)

Figure 6.8 *The Gay Year*, cover (1949)

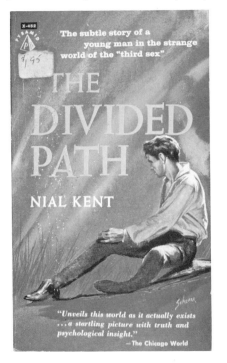

Figure 6.9 *The Divided Path*, cover (1951)

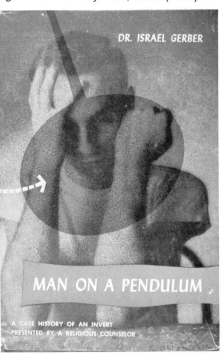

Figure 6.10 *Man on a Pendulum*, cover (1955)

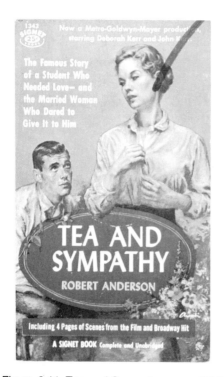

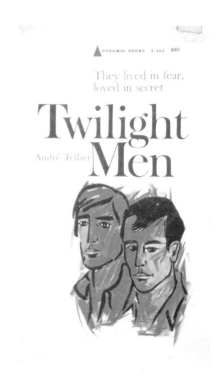

Figure 6.11 Tea and Sympathy, cover (1956)   Figure 6.12 Twilight Men, cover (1957)

Figure 6.13 The Heart in Exile, cover (1961)

Figure 6.14 *Maybe – Tomorrow*, cover (1965)

Figure 6.15 *Somewhere between the Two*, cover (1965)

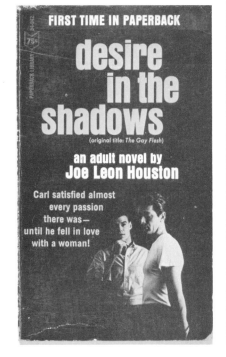

Figure 6.16 *Desire in the Shadows*, cover (1966)

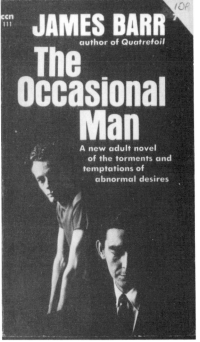

Figure 6.17 *The Occasional Man*, cover (1966)

The men depicted are young. Their youth is important in at least three respects. First of all, it provides a narrative tension to the image. Youth is a period of transition, of uncertain narrative outcome. In this context, outcome has to do not only with whether or not the young hero will have homosexual experience (that is more or less guaranteed) but whether he will turn out to be/become queer. Secondly, their youth is often part of their beauty. On the covers this seldom runs to the glowing descriptions inside but the use of averagely good-looking men (drawn or photographed) and the sometimes sensual use of light both indicate that the heroes of these books are to be found attractive. This attractiveness makes them figures for both identification (the better self often seen by fans in their chosen stars) and desire. In other words, as much as the image may be trumpeted as being about others, it is available to be taken as being about oneself, and as much as it is about a terrible, miserable way of being it also sets it up as an erotically desirable one. Thirdly, the peaking of this mode of gay representation in the 1940s, 1950s and 1960s must be read through the cultural energy invested in the period in the notion of youth, a key aspect of which was the successful transition to responsible adulthood. In principle this applied to women as much as men, but men were constructed as the main focus of anxiety. The worry was about whether boys would become successful, mature adult males; the possibility that they might turn out queer was one of the dangers along the way.

There are usually two men on the covers, sometimes touching, more often yearning towards each other. The feeling is pornographic in that it stresses the longing for physical consummation, but also romantic in its isolation of the couple. This catches exactly the emotional tone in which the sad young man has his being: romantic–pornographic.

The young men on the covers generally have a downcast gaze, the sign of melancholy. Unlike other young men of the 1950s, they are not 'angry'. The sadness in store for them has many dimensions – among others, the 'inevitable' short-lived nature of gay relationships, the lack of children, social opprobrium. An image of what the gay world is like is held up as the appalling prospect for the young chap. When he has his first contact with the gay scene he is generally repulsed (figure 6.18) and the image of the neurotic, hysterical, bitchy gay man as what the young man will become if he turns out to be/become queer haunts the image. Coming out – accepting that one is gay – thus takes the form of going in to another world ('cross[ing] over the border into the half-world of homosexuality' – *All the Sad Young Men*). This is striking in *Pink Narcissus*, which centres on a young man's sexual fantasies. He mooches about his apartment in various states of highly revealing dress, has various soft porn fantasies and towards the end invites a client into his room. The client, a pathetic old man, turns out to be himself, the terrible prospect of what he will become. The sad young man image is frozen on the moment before 'becoming' or knowing

Armand felt ill-at-ease with these men about him displaying the sides
of their natures that were usually so defended against the gaze of others.

Figure 6.18 Illustration from *Twilight Men*, 1957 edition

that one 'is' a queer, and the narrative usually either stresses the inevitable hatefulness of this destiny (from which one may be rescued by a good woman or death) or else allows the fantasy that after all one might meet an ordinary fellow like oneself and maybe, just maybe, live with him in bliss for the rest of one's life.

The settings on the covers are generally implicitly urban. The city is where homosexual encounters occur and many of the negative associations of urbanism with alienation are present. In the US examples the young man comes from outside the city, discovers the queer world there but generally still yearns for the unqueer homo-eroticism of encounters with the loved one by a secluded pool.

Finally, the lighting and/or colouring generally suggests evening, twilight, shadows. This may have sinister resonances, drawing as it does (at many removes) on expressionist Angst and Surrealist dreamscapes; it may also suggest traditions of chiaroscuro erotica or the dimmed lights of the Hollywood mise-en-scène for making a pass. The wording anchors these fluid feeling tones in the symbolic possibilities of twilight. This connotes sadness, the dying of the light and so on; it is also a period of transition, which here is not so much that of childhood to adulthood as between straight and gay worlds. The idea of a 'half-world' suggests both being in between the sexes and also not being a self-sufficient world, one without the connectives that make normal society so rich and satisfying.

> HANDSOME TERRY WALLACE LIVED IN THE TWILIGHT OF SEX BETWEEN THE DAYLIGHT OF NORMAL LOVE AND THE NIGHT OF FORBIDDEN DESIRE!
>
> (*Somewhere between the Two* (back cover))

> He had known infatuation, but this . . . this was different! Bigger than anything he'd ever felt before. And it did not seem 'unnatural'.
>
> (*The Divided Path* (back cover))

We don't really know what the relation is between a book and its cover, beyond the saw that we shouldn't use the latter as a basis for judgement. The cover sets up a tone, a promise of what we will find inside; it can be the reason why we buy the book and may be the filter of expectations through which, at least initially, we read it. Our desire that the book be like the cover may mean that we make it so as we read it, or are disappointed or pleasantly surprised to find it at variance to the cover. Particularly striking with the sad young man is the negative impression of the covers and the often far more upbeat and positive text inside, where the ectasy of homo-sexual love, the unfairness of social attitudes and the fun of camp culture are all to varying degrees suggested.

The explanation of the gap between cover and text is to be found not only in the habit of lying that necessarily defines advertising, nor even in the widespread pull between meeting a readership pleasure in the romantic/erotic and a moral guardian pressure group demand for rectitude. Equally important is the ambiguity over whom these books are for. One imagines that most, especially those with more salacious blurbs, are intended for a gay readership, but to be clear about that automatically grants gays a legitimacy as a reading constituency, which is tantamount to giving them/us the subject position of a full citizen. So the books have to come on as if addressing a straight readership informing them about 'them'. Thus *Maybe – Tomorrow* announces that *The Navy News Review* considered it 'a book adults should read if they truly want to know more about one of the little known segments of the human race', which implies that no one who actually belongs to that segment is being addressed. Interestingly *Somewhere between the Two* on its inside cover acknowledges that there may be more than one audience. Though it says the book 'will be an eye-opening revelation of the world of homosexuality that is all around *us'* (my italics), it also says that 'the search for physical love and emotional security' of the two main characters 'will be instantly understood by the countless other men who secretly live in the shadows of the twilight world of sex'.

> 'I wish I'd been born a cripple. They wouldn't set such store by my body then.'
>
> *(Twilight Men)*

Homi Bhabha (1983) has argued in the context of racial stereotyping that the fixity and stability of stereotypes is only apparent. Stereotypes are a function of the desire to control through knowledge; the stereotype, its fixed contours and endless repetition, constantly reassures 'us' that such-and-such a group is known – *this* is what slags or niggers or queers are like and every time we look, 'they' are still the same as 'we' always knew they were. Yet the *stereo*-typicality of the stereotype, the endless need to repeat it, betrays, suggests Bhabha, the underlying knowledge that in actuality no social group is fixed, really under the grasp of knowledge, and in particular, that relations of power are not static, that they have to be endlessly remade and reasserted, that the frozen, forever, already known quality of the way out-groups are seen is really a mask for realities that are disturbingly fluid, impermanent and never really known.

The need for stereotypes to represent social groups as if they are fixedly known should not be taken to mean that stereotypes are always images of stasis. Many stereotypes do indeed assert the static, unchanging, settled nature of the designated group – perhaps the mammy is one of the clearest instances. But stereotypes can also represent a state of impermanence or transience, and all age-based stereotypes must implicity do so, since no one remains the same age for ever. The sad young man is especially strongly marked in terms of transition, not only by virtue of age but also by virtue of the notion of moving between normal and queer worlds, always caught at the moment of exploration and discovery.

Other stereotypes that are mobilized in the context of the sad young man – especially that of the outrageous but miserable queen – do suggest a static personality, a known type whose main reassurance is his recognizability, his lack of the invisibility that in fact characterizes gay people. But the sad young man is not so fixed. Indeed, in relation to visibility, he both is and is not knowable from appearance. Sometimes sad young men are definitely effeminate, sissy, even, in *The Gay Year*, incipiently hermaphroditic (though when he eventually starts to turn straight, the hero observes that his shoulders have broadened and his chest has flattened), but much of the time it is not clear. The *Twilight Men* cover (figure 6.12) catches the middle point between *The Gay Year*'s over-neat, over-slim men and *Desire in the*

Shadows's utterly ordinary-looking youths. *Twilight Men*'s men are square jawed, with casual male haircuts, yet with lips perhaps rather too full, shirts rather too open and collars rather too generously 'set'; as is most usual with sad young men, you can't tell one (queer) from the other (normal) and yet there are always tell-tale signs – the fear over our invisibility is stated simultaneously with the reassurance that we are not invisible.

Both physically and narratively the sad young man is a stereotype of impermanence and transience. Returning to Bhabha's argument, what reassuring knowledge is there in this stereotype? What is the fluidity and ungaspability at issue in this image which is itself of an unresolved, uncertain identity?

What the sad young man stereotype delivers is the reassurance that there *will be* resolution and certainty. The world before the sad young man offers four resolutions: death, normality, becoming a dreadful old queen or, especially in the later texts, finding 'someone like oneself' with whom one can settle down. What this asserts is that the situation in which options are open, in which sexual identity is not fixed, will not last. In other words, the mutability of sexual desire and identity, its unruly unsettledness, need not trouble the social order after all because it is only a function of youth when of course things are uncertain and up for grabs. Policing and controlling the body through the proliferation of sexual categories requires that there is always going to be a fixing into category; the sad young man allows for an expression of the experience of libidinal fluidity while offering the reassurance that it will not last.

There is another dimension of reassurance, concerning heterosexual masculinity. All anxiety about adolescent males has to do with the contradictory definitions of real manliness, on the one hand asserted and reproduced through compulsory heterosexuality but on the other hand most intensely expressed in the women-excluding buddy system, in a profound inculcation of woman-hating and in the celebration of tearaway, freewheeling, undomesticated adventuring. The reconciliation of responsible heterosexual masculinity with buddy–buddy thrills and spills is a hard act and forms the tedious basis of many tales of heterosexuality.

The sad young man relates to this in contradictory ways. On the one hand, the yearning for sexual closeness could, worryingly, be part of a continuum with asexual buddiness (and has often been so interpreted, most famously by Fiedler (1960)). The sad young man is a reassurance that this is not so, that sexual love is not buddy love, that queers are not real men and, what a relief, real men are not queers. (Even when the hero wins the high school jock, as in *The Dividing Path* or *Maybe – Tomorrow*, still it is made clear that their relationship is not just buddiness carried on by other means but is different, more like man–woman 'love'.) On the other hand, very often the masculine ideal is held up by the texts as in fact unpleasant and undesirable. This is most explicitly worked through in *Tea and Sympathy*, where the hero is not homosexual though he is sad and sensitive; both play and film reassure him (us?) that one can be sensitive and hetero, that machismo is boring and often based on repressing homosexual feelings ('This was the weakness you cried out for me to save you from', says Laura to her determinedly homophobic husband at the climax of the play.) The unequivocality of an anti-machismo message could perhaps be made only in the context of denying that sensitivity in men goes hand in hand with homosexuality, but the message remains implicit in many of the other texts, where it is clear that normal masculinity is a far from attractive prospect. All of which suggests that for all the impulse in the stereotype to put us off being queer, the very worries that give rise to it – libidinal fluidity, the contradiction of masculinity – also betray the fact that it might be rather nice to be gay.

> There is probably no more sensitive individual anywhere than the homosexual, and yet, as a rule, he wouldn't be anything but a homosexual. He talks of being a member of an ill-treated minority, but he wouldn't sign up with the majority tomorrow.
>
> *(The Sixth Man)*

Stereotypes mean differently for different groups, and especially for those who are members of the stereotyped group as compared to those who are not. It is partly a matter of how you see it. Tessa Perkins (1979) uses the example of the stereotype of the scatterbrained housewife to make this point. This may be read as an indication of women's essentially irrational psyche but may also be understood as an acknowledgement that housewifery demands and develops a capacity to think of many things at once, to keep on the go from one to another. The title of one of the first gay liberationist films, *It is not the Homosexual who is Perverse, but the Situation in which he Finds Himself* says it all, and the film in part takes the form of the sexual political education of a sad young man who comes to realize that if he is unhappy it is not because of himself but because of social oppression. The possibility of reading queer unhappiness in these terms is glimpsed even in the most homophobic of sad young man texts ('Don't be dejected, John. If only society were set up differently . . .' – *Man on a Pendulum*) and it must have been an available reading strategy in the years of emergent gay militancy and eventual law reform.

Equally the sad young man is a figure of romance/pornography. The image of handsome men nearly touching one another in sensual half-light is clearly titillating as are descriptions of a man 'endowed with a magnificent body and stunning good looks' (*Somewhere between the Two*) or the casting of full-lipped Sal Mineo in *Rebel without a Cause* and fresh-faced John Kerr in *Tea and Sympathy*. A characteristic feature of gay/lesbian fantasy is the possibility of oscillation between wanting to be and want-ing to have the object of desire. In heterosexual fantasy, the (always female) nurse is not supposed to want to be the (always male) doctor, the female reader is not supposed to lust after the heirs of Jane Eyre nor the male reader to fancy his out-of-focus substitute in porn maga-zines. Actual reading practices are always more complicated and inse-cure than this, but desiring both to be the object of desire and to want the subject of desire structures the text of lesbian/gay fantasy. The sad young man is the subject of desire of these texts; he longs for handsome guys that we are encouraged to fancy too; but writing or imaging also encourages us to fancy the sad young man himself. This could amount to a celebration of homosexual love. If we are turned on by the men he is turned on by, that means we share and, if only during the reading/viewing, endorse his desire; and if we think he is desirable because handsome and admirable because sensitive, then we also endorse being him. For all the bad feelings he has about himself, we could feel pretty good about him.

I don't want to overstate the scope of putative positive gay readings. The delicious melancholia in the presentation of the type was generally allied to social passivity, a sense that nothing could be done about social unfairness, that we had always been persecuted. Because it was about the sad *young* man, the pleasures of identifying with him were themselves wistful, for the sadness was that one could not go on being him and that wanting him when you'd stopped being him would be a pathetic business. The image could seldom really shake free from all this, yet it did con-struct a sense of feeling good about queer desire. If at one extreme it represented a warning of misery, which a gay man could have laid at the door of his ineradicable pervertedness, at the other it offered an image of holy sensitivity, stunning good looks, overwhelming erotic experience and escape from the dreariness of real manliness, for all of which a gay man may have felt that some unreasonable, socially induced suffering was a small price to pay.

> Julian was incapable of changing, perhaps because inversion was a deeply ingrained habit with him, but largely because he found love for a man a beautiful and exciting mystery.
>
> (*The Heart in Exile*)

NOTES

1 Ballet choreographed by Rudi van Dantzig and first performed by the Dutch National Ballet in Amsterdam in 1965; description from Jackson 1978: 38.
2 Film by Willard Maas made in 1948; description from Durgnat 1972: 252.
3 'Ce corps d'athlète gracieusement déhanché, percé de flèches, comme aban-

donnés dans une agonie délicieuse et lascive, je conçois sans peine que des générations de jeunes hommes épris, dans le secret de leur coeur, de leurs semblables, l'aient caressé du regard, palpant chacun des ses muscles.' Castello 1983: 13–15.

4 See Steakley 1975 and Weeks 1977.

REFERENCES

Becker, Raymond de (1967) *The Other Face of Love*, London: Neville Spearman & Rodney Books.

Bhabha, Homi (1983) 'The Other Question – the Stereotype and Colonial Discourse', *Screen* 24 (6): 18–36.

Castello, Michel del (1983) 'Le Plaisir de mourir', in *Saint Sébastien: Adonis et Martyr*, Paris: Persona.

Cooper, Emmanuel (1986) *The Sexual Perspective*, London: Routledge & Kegan Paul.

Durgnat, Raymond (1972) *Sexual Alienation in the Cinema*, London: Studio Vista.

Fiedler, Leslie (1960) *Love and Death in the American Novel*, New York: Criterion.

Jackson, Graham (1978) *Dance as Dance*, Ontario: Catalyst.

Moon, Michael (1987) ' "The Gentle Boy from the Dangerous Classes": Pederasty, Domesticity, and Capitalism in Horatio Alger', *Representations* 19: 87–110.

Perkins, T. E. (1979) 'Rethinking Stereotypes', in Michèle Barrett, Philip Corrigan, Annette Kuhn and Janet Wolff (eds) *Ideology and Cultural Production*, London: Croom Helm, 135–60.

Springhall, John (1983–4) 'The Origins of Adolescence', *Youth and Policy* 2 (3): 20–35.

Steakley, James (1975) *The Homosexual Emancipation Movement in Germany*, New York: Arno.

Weeks, Jeffrey (1977) *Coming Out*, London: Quartet.

SAD YOUNG MEN TEXTS

Books

The reference given is for first publication which may be different from the edition of which the cover is discussed and illustrated.

Anderson, Robert *Tea and Sympathy*, New York: Random House (1953).

Anon. *All the Sad Young Men*, New York: Wisdom House (1962).

Baldwin, James *Giovanni's Room*, New York: Dial (1956).

De F., M. *The Gay Year*, New York: Castle Books (1949).

Garland, Rodney *The Heart in Exile*, London: W. H. Allen (1953).

Gerber, Israel *Man on a Pendulum*, New York: The American Press (1955).

Kent, Nial *The Divided Path*, New York: Greenberg (1949).

Little, Jay *Maybe – Tomorrow*, New York: Pageant Press (1952).

Little, Jay *Somewhere between the Two*, New York: Pageant Press (1956).

Niles, Blair *Strange Brother*, New York: Liveright (1931).

Stearn, Jess *The Sixth Man*, New York: Doubleday (1961).

Tellier, André *Twilight Men*, New York: Greenberg (1931).

Vidal, Gore *The City and the Pillar*, New York: E. P. Dutton (1948).

Films

Advise and Consent (USA 1962); d. Otto Preminger.
Boys in the Band, The (USA 1969–70); d. William Friedkin.
Fragment of Seeking (USA 1946–7); d. Curtis Harrington.
Images in the Snow (USA 1948); d. Willard Maas.
Leather Boys, The (GB 1964); d. Sidney Furie.
Lot in Sodom (USA 1930); d. Melville Webber and James Sibley Watson.
L-Shaped Room, The (GB 1962); d. Bryan Forbes.
Passing Strangers (USA 1974); d. Arthur Bressan.
Pink Narcissus (USA 1971); d. Anon.
Rebel without a Cause (GB 1955); d. Nicholas Ray.
Strange One, The (USA 1957); d. Jack Garfein.
Taste of Honey, A (GB 1961); d. Tony Richardson.
Tea and Sympathy (USA 1956); d. Vincente Minnelli.
Twice a Man (USA 1962–3); d. Gregory Markopoulos.
Victim (GB 1961); d. Basil Dearden.
Voices, The (USA 1953); d. John Smitz.

FURTHER READING

Austen, Roger (1977) *Playing the Game: the Homosexual Novel in America*, New York: Bobbs–Merrill.
Curtin, Kaier (1987) *'We Can Always Call Them Bulgarians': the Emergence of Lesbians and Gay Men on the American Stage*, Boston: Alyson.
Dyer, Richard (1977) *Now You See It: Studies in Lesbian and Gay Film*, London: Routledge.
Russo, Vito (1981) *The Celluloid Closet: Homosexuality in the Movies*, New York: Harper & Row.
Sarotte, Georges–Michel (1978) *Like a Brother, Like a Lover*, Garden City, NY: Doubleday.

Chapter 7

Victim: hegemonic project

This is an approach to *Victim* in terms of its historical/cultural significance. It attracts my attention in the first place because of my involvement in the gay movement and because it was, in gay terms, a first – the first film to defend homosexuality as a cause in a mainstream context, the first to deal with gayness explicitly (earlier examples demand a good deal of 'reading in'), the first to have a major star playing a gay character.[1] In trying to work out the significance of *Victim* as a first, I have thought of it not as an expression of some vague Zeitgeist or cultural world-view, nor as a 'stimulus' which had a discernable 'effect' on the law, public attitudes or the daily lives of gay people, but rather as a way of intervening – a way characteristic of British cinema – in a social debate. I try to see the making and watching of *Victim* as social activities. In other words, I shall not be treating *Victim* as the sum of its influences (e.g. film conventions, the work of Relph, Dearden, Green and Bogarde), though I shall be discussing these; nor in terms of how people were influenced by it, though I shall be suggesting ways in which we can conceptualize this; but rather examining *Victim* as a particular characteristic organization of codes and conventions which gives warrant for certain kinds of reading on the part of its audience, that is, a particular set of encodings which makes possible particular decodings. Encoding and decoding are social practices. I try to keep in mind throughout the Marxist formula: 'People (film-makers, audiences) make their own history (films), but not in circumstances of their own choosing'.

The project of a film like *Victim* is to create a 'unified' or 'organic' artefact. Virtually all art everywhere has just this project, and it virtually always involves the suppression or omission of contradictions and disruptions of various kinds. This project represents a bid for hegemony, which I understand as the expression of the interests and world-views of a particular social group or class so expressed as to pass for the interest and world-view of the whole of society. Hegemony is something that a class, gender and/or race constantly has to work for – it is never permanently, statically established in a culture. It seems to me likely that the degree to which the suppression of contradictions in an art-work actually shows is a register of the hold of a particular hegemony at the moment of the film's production. Where there is a sense of strain at holding down contradiction, I would posit either the ruling groups' own lack of faith in their world-view (contradictions *within* dominant ideology) or the presence in other groups of a hard and disturbing challenge to the ruling groups' hegemony (contradictions *to* dominant ideology). In the case of *Victim*, I am going to argue that there is a sense of strain, though not a very great one, in a film of in some ways quite remarkable unity, and that this is due in small part to contradictions within the dominant ideology of the film, but in larger part to the fact that by taking on the subject matter of homosexuality the film takes on objective contradictions to dominant ideology, which had not however, in 1961, been marshalled into an active challenge to that ideology.

PROJECT

The notion of the 'organic' or 'unified' film was widespread in British film theory before 1961. Writers such as Ernest Lindgren (1948), Roger Manvell (1944) and Paul Rotha (1948) all invoke it, unquestioningly, in their description of how a good film is, or should be. Rotha in particular is strikingly prescriptive:

> a film should be distinguished by a unity of purpose and should be single-minded in intention . . .
>
> . . . by utilising the means arising out of the nature of the medium itself, the film sets out to be a form of expression, presenting persons, objects and incidents in a way entirely different from any other medium . . .
>
> Montage may be understood as the inclusive, creative and constructive unity that is present from the birth of the first gleam of idea in the mind of the scenarist, to the final act of assembling the film strips by constructive editing and cutting.
>
> (ibid.: 338, 345)

This is familiar enough. Another word for 'organic' is 'closed', as defined for instance by Peter Wollen in his article 'Counter Cinema: *Vent d'est*' (1972) and seen by much writing in *Screen* in the 1970s and early 1980s as typifying virtually all cinema. The Rotha book was a particularly influential text, and written by a representative of a particularly influential movement, documentary. Apart from the general insistence on unity, it also draws attention to the peculiarly British insistence on the importance of technique, the specifically cinematic, in the realization of unity, and the special stress on montage. In the passage quoted, Rotha gives a very broad definition to montage, but later he makes it clear that the final stage of editing is decisive; and while British montage may not be exactly what the

Russian formalists envisioned, it does certainly go beyond the invisible joins of standard narrative cinema. (Think, for instance, of the use of editing in documentary, as discussed by Lovell and Hillier (1972), rhythmic editing in films such as *I Know Where I'm Going* and *Brief Encounter*, Hammer films' development of the shock cut.)

In terms of narrative organization, *Victim* is remarkably organic/closed. It is, firstly, rounded off in the two ways that mainstream cinema leads us to expect: the crime is solved (and the culprit caught) and the heterosexual couple is, however awkwardly, united. Secondly, the organization of suspense follows two set patterns – firstly, a series of acts by one character, Jack Barratt (running from the police, ringing Farr, seeing various people, stuffing something down a lavatory), whose connection is concealed from the audience until the all-explaining revelation that he was gay; then, a second mystery, about who the blackmailer is. We are given a couple of false trails (a gay couple, PH and Mickie (figure 7.1), and a man in a bowler hat, Hoey); but we are also introduced to the mastermind (the bookshop assistant, Miss Benham) – and twice the film cuts directly from the innocent suspects, the gay couple, to the guilty Miss Benham. Both false trails and guilty party are securely yanked into the narrative organization. PH and Mickie know Barratt and are regulars at the film's gay pub, the Checkers; they are in fact the first gay characters we see (apart from Barratt and Farr). Hoey, who chats up Barratt's friend, Eddy, turns out to be a policeman, and is instrumental in nailing Miss Benham. The bookshop where the latter works also serves as the link between Farr, the crusader against blackmail, and Farr, the gay man implicated in the blackmail – the bookshop is where Barratt lived with the owner Harold before falling in love with Farr; when Farr goes to pay the blackmail in the bookshop, he has to face also Harold's jealousy and distress. Miss Benham's identification with the bookshop awkwardly draws the narrative strings together.

Apparent unity is further achieved by the way that nearly all the minor characters turn out to be relevant to the central narrative – Farr's friends, Fullbrook and Mandrake, turn out to be gay, and are friends of actor Calloway (figure 7.2), who has his hair done at Henry's, who gives his name to Farr after being beaten up by the blackmailer's assistant, Sandy. Farr knows Henry because Eddy, a crony at the Checkers and flatmate of Barratt, gave Farr his name. 'Fag-hag' Madge buys rounds for everyone at the Checkers on the strength of working for Mandrake, gay friend of Fullbrook, Calloway and Farr. Phil, the car salesman who will not help the fugitive Barratt, but later does help Farr in tracking down the blackmailers, has also been working for the latter, providing them with names when he no longer had money for what they had on him. We've already noted the way Harold, Miss Benham and Hoey dovetail into the plot, though, like the others, initially introduced as local colour.

All this is so neat that its very facticity might – and to some probably

Figure 7.1 Victim: PH and Mickie, queer false leads

does – become apparent. However, the mechanism of suspense probably imposes a unity, or control, over the events that may be more powerful than questions of likelihood or coincidence. As Thomas Elsaesser has noted in the context of the American cinema:

> This special case [suspense] of the dramatic continuum – special in that it presents evidence of an accelerated sense of causality and fatalism – operates occasionally at the expense of plausibility and verisimilitude. For the creation of suspense can often have a unifying force which successfully overplays plot-weaknesses and schematic characters.
>
> (1971: 9)

In addition, three other elements – the use of technique, the relation of the tight construction to a view of the gay world, and a certain surface realism – all work to mask the over-schematic workings of the narrative.

There is a technical expertise in the construction of *Victim* that conforms to Rotha's prescriptions for film. All the techniques at the film-makers'

Figure 7.2 Victim: Fullbrook, Calloway and Farr, all queer

disposal are used to bind the narrative together into a self-sufficient whole. In particular montage, understood not just as editing but as the use of technique to stress connections between images, is widely used to pull the elements together. Camera movement, for instance, is used not for its kinaesthetic effect but in order to draw attention to links between various elements in the mise-en-scène (understood here as dress, decor, setting and actors). To take just one example – at the end of the scene where Sandy is sitting phoning his blackmail accomplice, to the sound of a classical gramophone record, agreeing to put the screws on Farr, he puts the phone down and exits, punching a punch-ball as he does; the camera follows him from the chair to the punch-ball and then carries on to a photograph of Michelangelo's *David* on the wall. Punchball and David had always been in shot, but the camera movement links them together with Sandy's movement, suggesting a connection of athleticism and aestheticism that is one of the paradigms in the straight imagination of homosexuality. The film does not follow up this hint about Sandy, yet this montage-through-camera-movement seems to suggest that it is an element of characterization that is integral to the film. Editing proper works in similar ways.

For instance, Laura is at the children's home watching a boy painting a face; a doctor observes how well the boy is coming on, thanks to Laura; she sits down, and reads in the paper of Barratt's suicide; her face darkens; cut to the boy furiously drawing strokes through his painting, disfiguring it. This is a particularly typical example of British montage editing. Clearly it is a cut that serves no narrative function. However, unlike the Russian fomalists, it also has no intellectual function either – it is purely affective. In addition, it has been carefully naturalized. Unlike the lions at Odessa in *Battleship Potemkin*, whose 'arbitrariness' V. F. Perkins has discussed (1972: 103–5), this boy is part of the setting; he has not been dragged in from another place in time and space. Yet he is also arbitrary in many ways – why, after all, does he suddenly start disfiguring his painting? It is the use of crudely emotive, yet naturalized, cutting in of images that is characteristic of British cinema. What is additionally interesting in this example is the fact that it is apparently unmotivated, and the fact that it is a child. Children are important motifs in *Victim*, yet they also, as we shall see, raise issues the film cannot handle. It is not surprising that the film's expertise flounders just when, as I shall argue, it is really on to something.

The closed coherence of *Victim* – in so far as the strains of coincidence and wilfully expert montage don't show – neatly resumes an assumption about the structure of the gay world: namely, that it is a tight-knit, highly delimited cross-class underworld. It is doubtful whether producers and audiences alike could believe that an ordinary brown envelope with an address label on it could immediately indicate that the addressee was being blackmailed for being gay, that Eddy would be bound to stumble across the others who were being blackmailed, or that there could be close links of friendship between such social unequals as a builder's labourer, a lawyer, a bookseller, a car salesman, a lord, a hairdresser, a star actor and an artist, were it not for an ideology of credibility that maintained that just such a close meshing of individuals and circumstances characterized the gay underworld. In particular, consorting across class barriers was a major feature of the discussion of trials from Wilde to Peter Wildeblood, and preoccupies the authors of novels like Rodney Garland's *The Heart in Exile* (1953) and the anonymous *A Room in Chelsea Square* (1956).

Into this tightly-bound microcosm the agents of the law, the police and the courts have to be inserted. Here the first real ambiguities of the film begin to emerge. Verbally, the law is presented as being outside of the gay world, an impartial arbiter in its relations with the blackmailers. Thus the police chief is given the film's message to state: 'There's no doubt that a law that sends homosexuals to prison offers unlimited opportunities for blackmail', and at the end of the film, when the opposition of the two crimes (homosexuality and blackmail) is raised with him, he says, 'I'm a policeman – I don't have feelings'. Similarly Farr, as a lawyer, confronted with the fact of his upper-class friends' gayness and attendant persecution says,

'I'm a lawyer – I don't make the law, I practise it'. Even here there is the disquieting note of possibility that a law may be wrong; but what the lines serve to emphasize is the impartiality of law enforcement, its separateness from the phenomenon it investigates and prosecutes. Yet characterization belies the affirmations. Firstly and most importantly, Farr, representative of the law, is also gay and therefore guilty before the law. (Strictly speaking, the film is at pains to avoid the full impact of this issue by insisting that Farr has never, since marrying, acted on his desires – even the incriminating photograph is profitable to the blackmailers only by virtue of the love in Farr's eyes as he looks at the weeping Barratt.) This is a point I shall return to. Secondly, the police chief declares his lack of emotion seconds after needlessly punching Phil in fury for his cowardly involvement with the blackmailers. Thirdly, there is the character of the detective Bridie who expresses distrust and distaste for homosexuals, and whose anti-gay brusqueness and contempt is kept in line only by the 'blokeish' wisdom of the chief. Fourthly, and most ambiguously, there is the character of the plainclothes policeman Hoey, whose identity as a policeman is revealed only in the final sequence of the film (when he observes who picks up Farr's blackmail money in the bookshop). Before this he has been depicted as a shy, bowler-hatted regular at the Checkers, who eyes up Eddy and eventually asks him to have a coffee. At one level, this is just one of the 'surprises' that the script sets up – the philanthropic Lord Fullbrook turns out to be gay, PH and Mickie are con men, Hoey is a policeman. This plays upon the 'hidden' or 'invisible' quality of homosexuality – you can never tell who is and who isn't. Perhaps it was meant to be no more than this; but we are surely entitled to ask just what he has been doing in the Checkers, going so far as to chat up Eddy. Surely – and Eddy's suspicious, though interested, response might support this – Hoey is also an agent provocateur. That is, the film begins to open up – but not, of course, to explore – the fact that not only is the law possibly unjust and its practitioners emotionally or prejudicially involved, but that also the law actually roots out, by trickery if need be, victims for prosecution. The law's verbal declarations are contradicted by what its enforcers do.

The relation of the law to the gay world raises one further point. The film is organized around the investigation of crime (theft, then blackmail) and the agents of investigation are the agents of the law. This means that the victim image (victims of blackmail, victims of the law) is reinforced by the gay characters' narrative passivity. They do occasionally help – Eddy noting Henry and Phil's sense of fear, Henry phoning Farr to give him Calloway's name – but by and large they are, as the police chief says, 'little people' who can do nothing. The gay characters are thus robbed of any active role in shaping their lives or their world. Except, once again, for Farr . . .

The final element that tries to enforce a coherent vision in the film is a certain form of 'realism'. This works at two levels. Firstly, it provides some additional cues to the film's veracity. The use of location shooting and the topicality of the subject matter act as 'guarantees' that the film is not mere fabrication, as does the acting of the minor roles. These last are played by actors drawn from the limited and familiar repertory of 'character actors', developed especially at Ealing (where director Basil Dearden and producer Michael Relph worked) but also throughout the British film industry. In this repertory, minor bit-players (who in comedy could be principals) developed a particular 'character' of their own, comparable to that embodied by major stars in Hollywood. In this way, the roles they play are both familiar and also both broader and more individuated than a pure stereotype, drawing on a connotative range beyond the film in question and yet not straying into the realms of 'psychological' explorations (the 'rounded character') or social naturalism. Given too a certain widespread belief in the success of Ealing's 'projection of British character', the contribution to *Victim* of performers such as Dennis Price, John Barrie, Noel Howlett, Frank Pettit, Mavis Villiers, Charles Lloyd Pack, Norman Bird and Margaret Diamond (though their *names* may not have been familiar) helped the attempt to enforce a certain authoritative credibility.

Secondly, this realism, and especially the character actors, helped the film to deal with the question of class. To understand this, we have first to understand the type of film *Victim* is.

Victim was one of a cycle of British commercial feature films dealing with social issues or problems. This cycle dates as far back as 1947 with *Frieda* (about an English man married to a German woman), although the years in which it was strongest are roughly 1956–63. The films of this cycle share many of the features I have described in *Victim* – unity imposed through narrative construction and 'montage' (as defined by Rotha *et al.*), use of character actors and location shooting. Not all the films in this cycle, however, are as adept as *Victim*. What really links them, in addition to the peculiarity of raising social issues in a commercial form, is the way in which they define social problems *vis-à-vis* class. For on the one hand they show, through attention to setting and through the class nuances established by the character actors, considerable awareness of variation in class while at the same time effectively denying any conflict or struggle between classes.

Within the British cinema, the social problem feature film dominated the definition of what constituted a social problem; and the issues it focused on were those that have traditionally been thought of as being 'outside of' history, and therefore class struggle – that is to say, sex and the family. The largest category of problems dealt with in these films is youth: *My Teenage Daughter* (1956), *Violent Playground* (1957), *The Young and the Guilty* (1958), *The Lady is a Square* (1958), *Too Young to Love* (1959), *Serious Charge* (1959), *Spare the Rod* (1961), *Some People* (1962), *The Wild and the Willing* (1962), *Term of Trial* (1962), *That Kind of Girl* (1963), *The*

Party's Over (1963), *The System* (1964). As Clarke, Hall, Jefferson and Roberts argue in *Sub-cultures, Cultures and Class* (1975), these years mark the development of a real but class-specific phenomenon in society, youth culture, that is however concurrently defined by the mass media exclusively in terms of youth, suppressing the dimension of class. The second major category (which includes some of the same films) deals with sexual deviations or problems – prostitution: *The Flesh Is Weak* (1956), *Passport to Shame* (1957), *The L-Shaped Room* (1962), *The Yellow Teddybears* (1963), *The World Ten Times Over* (1963); pederasty: *Serious Charge* (1959), *Never Take Sweets from a Stranger* (1960), *The Mark* (1961); rape, as a problem for the rapist: *Don't Talk to Strange Men* (1962); venereal disease: *Too Young to Love* (1959), *That Kind of Girl* (1963); artificial insemination: *A Question of Adultery* (1958); impotence: *During One Night* (1960) and homosexuality, both female: *So Evil So Young* (1960), *The L-Shaped Room* (1962), *The World Ten Times Over* (1963), and male: *Victim* (1961), *The L-Shaped Room* (1962), *The Leather Boys* (1963), *The Pleasure Girls* (1965). Other films dealt with children – fostering: *The Divided Heart* (1954), *Girl on Approval* (1961); childlessness: *Lost* (1955); child welfare officers: *A Cry from the Streets* (1958); the dangers of drugs that look like sweets: *The Silent Playground* (1964); race: *Sapphire* (1959), *The Wind of Change* (1960), *Flame in the Streets* (1961) and slums and slum clearance: *No Trees in the Street* (1958), *A Place to Go* (1963). *Life for Ruth* (1962) dealt with the issue of religious objections to blood transfusion.

Women are particularly important in the cycle, which relates to 'the basic opposition which places man inside history, and woman as ahistoric and eternal' (Johnston 1973). The cycle's major narrative structures hinge on women – for example, the story of the young girl who is lured to the glitter of the city and is corrupted by it (*The Flesh is Weak, Passport to Shame, Too Young to Love, That Kind of Girl, Bitter Harvest, The World Ten Times Over* and *The Pleasure Girls*) – though the films are very unclear as to how much is the corruption of the city and how much is perversity in the girl; and thriller structures in which a woman is revealed as the culprit, such as *Lost, Wicked as they Come, Sapphire, Serious Charge* and *Victim*. There are also several films set in women's prisons or borstals: *The Weak and the Wicked, Yield to the Night, So Evil So Young*. By assigning these key roles to women in the narrative, the films reinforce the notion that these social problems are outside society.

The cycle was one in which Dearden and Relph were particularly involved, directing and producing *Frieda, Violent Playground, Sapphire, Victim, Life for Ruth, A Place to Go* and other related films. (*The League of Gentlemen* 1960 has a gallery of social outcasts, including a homosexual man; *The Mind Benders* 'tackled' brainwashing; and so on.) Janet Green also scripted *Sapphire, Victim* and *Life for Ruth* (with John McCormick).

Victim then is not a one-off, but a typical example of a socially conscious feature film. It fits into a tradition that notably avoids issues of class struggle not only by not dealing with issues such as strikes and profits but by not relating the issues dealt with to the specificities of class. In other words, homosexuality – or prostitution, or venereal disease, or youth – is seen to be essentially the same issue regardless of social class or economic circumstances. Yet in so class-ridden, class-conscious a society as Britain, class cannot actually be ignored. What these films do then is to present the phenomenal forms of class, through character acting and attention to details of dress and setting, while denying the real conflictual significance of class. Indeed the very acknowledgement of and attention paid to class differences often serves, paradoxically, to reinforce the assertion of their irrelevance to the real issue of the film. *Sapphire* for instance, upon which *Victim* is consciously modelled, insists on showing us black society as mirroring the class divisions of white society in order to stress the primacy of racial prejudice (reciprocal between blacks and whites) in racial conflict, rather than concrete inequalities. By giving as the look of class – self-consciously 'well-observed' – the films attain a true-to-life gloss, but by defining as *the* problems problems that are conceived of as being outside of class and history, the films avoid the struggle inherent in class society.

CONTRADICTIONS

Victim's project was to make a unified statement about homosexuality, employing strategies of tight narrative construction, enclosing montage and surface realism. As a strategy it looks fairly successful, though there are hints of strain in the editing, and in the role of the agents of the law in the narrative. The latter however is no small point. For the single fact that most seriously threatens the wholeness of *Victim*'s statement is the fact that its main character, who is acted by a major star, is at one and the same time an agent of the law and its victim, a subject and an object of the narrative organization. This means that the film cannot keep the issue of gayness at a distance (as *Sapphire* could with race). Moreover, Bogarde's decision to play the part, and to insist upon the character's own gayness being spelt out, forces the film to stumble over certain objective contradictions that it might otherwise have kept at bay. A positive view of homosexuality involves granting legitimacy to deviance, seeing sex as a source of pleasure rather than of procreation and validating sexual relationships outside compulsory monogamy. These are not positions the film wishes to endorse. With Bogarde as a heterosexual, liberal campaigner it need not have encountered them; but with him as homosexual it has to, however obliquely and confusedly.

The film is at considerable pains to keep the worlds of normalcy (the Farrs) and of deviance (the gay world) iconographically distinct. The Farrs are normal partly because they are stars, Dirk Bogarde and Sylvia Syms. Like most stars since the 1930s, they resolve the contradictions between two of the major social pressures of this society that people be highly individuated individuals and that people be one of the crowd. By existing as real people (not just as characters in fiction), existing moreover in a manner assumed to be largely identical with that of their screen personae, stars 'guarantee' the possibility of resolving this contradiction. They are both special and just like you or me. It is thus a commonplace paradox that two such well-heeled, well-groomed, attractive and articulate people as Bogarde and Syms should also represent ordinariness or normalcy. This is reinforced by the dull propriety of their places of work (the law chambers, the school) and the unfussy, streamlined 'good taste' of their home (the iconographic set drawn on here overlaps with that of the smartly dressed-down style of the royal family).

This world contrasts strikingly with the deviant (that is, gay) world even at the level of the Farrs' social equals. Bogarde's elegant quiff contrasts with Calloway (Dennis Price) removing his wig; the plain good taste of the Farr household is very different from the baroque arty-craftyness of Mandrake's mews flat; even their jobs underline the difference – straight lawyer and teacher as against deviant bohemian artist and actor (Lord Fullbrook's profession is not mentioned). Lower down the social scale there is a certain, albeit muted, emphasis on deformity in the gay world – PH is blind, the last shots of Barratt use chiaroscuro lighting effects, Harold is shot from below to emphasize his hang-dog features and pebble glasses. Emotive montage is used to bring a scene to a close on an image of gays distorted with fear – close-ups of Phil's hand furiously turning a pipe over and over, and of Henry's face screaming and crying as Sandy starts to smash the shop.

There is also an attempt to dissociate Bogarde from the gay world verbally as well as visually. He assures Laura that he has not broken his vow to her (i.e. he has not slept with a man since their marriage); he tells Fullbrook, Mandrake and Calloway that although he shares their 'instincts' he has always resisted them. Yet various elements – aspects of narrative, the Bogarde image, the notion of 'nature' – undermine the neatness of the separation. There are first of all such points as the blackmail photograph that we never see (we are told it shows only Barratt crying and love in Farr's eyes, but we are told this only at the end and are bound to make more lurid assumptions about it before this), the climax of the centrally placed scene between the Farrs, where he shouts at her that he stopped seeing Barratt 'because I *wanted* him', and the hints of a disastrous affair in his past (with 'young Stainer'), about which he is tauntingly reminded after his declaration that he has always resisted his impulses.

This contrast between the urbane exterior and hints of something darker beneath the surface is very much in line with Bogarde's image as it had developed up to this point. He was a pin-up, associated in a whole run of studio portraits with the gentlemanly life: large garden, riding horses, refined interiors, cavalry twills and cravats. He was a romantic lead and straight man in the *Doctor* films, and had had a huge success in the archetypal love weepie *The Wind Cannot Read* (1958) (as a young officer falling in love with a Japanese woman dying of leukaemia). In these ways he was a straightforward, heart-throb star in a British tradition going back through James Mason and Laurence Olivier to Leslie Howard and Ronald Colman. Yet the darker note was a persistent feature of his career. There were intimations of homosexuality in several of his previous roles: *Rope* on television (1947), *The Spanish Gardener* (1956), *The Singer not the Song* (1961), possibly *Hunted* (1952) and *Ill Met by Moonlight* (1957). He had also been set to play T. E. Lawrence in 1959. His early roles had combined youthful good looks with elements of criminality, sadism (in his treatment of girlfriends) and masochism (in the image of him wounded or on the run) – *The Blue Lamp* (1949), *Hunted* (1953), *The Gentle Gunman* (1952), *Desperate Moment* (1954), *The Spanish Gardener*; while later roles associated him with neurotic Romantic temperaments – *A Tale of Two Cities* (1958) as Sydney Carton, *Libel* (1959), *Song Without End* (1960) as Liszt. In addition, even in very straightforward films his acting style suggests repression of feeling, often manifested as an uneasy combination of cool, poised stretches of acting and sudden outbursts of anger. Thus Bogarde-as-Farr is a far more ambivalent, disquieting figure than the role as it is written might indicate; and the sense of repression that informs image and acting style reinforces repression motifs that I shall discuss in a moment.

This ambivalence extends to Farr's place *vis-à-vis* the film's overt (i.e. verbally stated) view of homosexuality. This is a play, endemic to discussion of the subject, on the notion of 'nature'. All the gay characters are made to insist that their being gay is their 'nature', is 'natural', and, furthermore, that this being so it is proper that they should 'follow their instincts'. Yet if no character is made to state that gayness is not natural, the notion that it may be a natural deformity is allowed for. There is some visual implication of this, as already suggested; Henry says 'Nature's played me a dirty trick' in reference to his gayness; and the barman at the Checkers tells Madge that if it is a part of nature then it is a 'sick and twisted part'. One can hardly berate *Victim* for being unable to pick its way through the conundrums that the fuzzy notion of nature as applied to human behaviour inevitably raises, but because the debate is set up in these terms (and suppressing the alternative term, 'culture'), Farr is in a double bind situation. For to have 'acted on his instincts' would have been to skirt sickness and deformity; yet not so to act, to suppress his instincts, is also 'unnatural'. That this implication is possible might however have gone unnoticed, were it not for the presentation of Laura and their marriage, the handling, that is, of monogamy and procreation.

Laura and Melville Farr are the ideal/ordinary married couple. They end that way too – except that Laura has to accept a non-sexual role in the marriage, and they are childless. That is, in terms of an ideology of nature and acting on nature, they are a most unnatural couple. It is the unnatural-ness of the couple, *including* Laura, that draws attention to the unnatural-ness of Melville not only for being gay but also for not acting on it. We could perhaps accept Laura's suppression of her own sexuality for the sake of her husband – such sacrifices are so much part and parcel of the cinema's, and the culture's, view of women, even in 1961. Indeed, women *not* like that constitute a 'social problem' category, as the social conscience feature cycle makes clear. What we would be less likely to accept was that she should accept being childless. The film nowhere has her mention her childlessness, yet children are a structuring absence in *Victim*.

The notion of a text's 'structuring absence' is a suggestive, even beguil-ing one, which is also much open to abuse. It does not mean things which are simply not in the text, or which the critic thinks ought to be in the text. The example above – the absence of class struggle from the text – is not an instance of a structuring absence; class struggle is simply not there, is not part of the film's terms of reference. A structuring absence on the other hand refers to an issue, or even a set of facts or an argument, that a text cannot ignore, but which it deliberately skirts round or otherwise avoids, thus creating the biggest 'holes' in the text, fatally, revealingly misshaping the organic whole assembled with such craft.

Victim's structuring absence is identifiable because the text is endlessly pointing towards it, almost obsessively making reference to it. Children recur again and again as images. Laura works with children; when she reads of Barratt's death, a boy she is supervising destroys his painting; when Melville comes to tell her of his decision to fight the blackmailers, he does so at the school, first in the playground, then in a deserted school-room which is invaded by yelling children before they have really finished speaking. In both these cases there is something violent about the chil-dren's eruption on the scene. Another such example occurs when Melville leaves the police station having learnt of Barratt's suicide, and a group of children on roller-skates clatters past him. Key moments in the plot are signalled by children. Yet, significantly, the only character in the film to have a child is Laura's brother, Scott, and we never see his son. To have shown him would have been to tackle head-on the 'abnormality' of Laura and Melville's marriage, whereas it is left to these nagging images to raise the spectre.

These images gain some importance from the place of children in the social conscience cycle. As an image of 'life', of 'the future', of 'hope', of 'continuity', they recur again and again, within the cycle (e.g. *Spare the Rod, Flame in the Streets, Life for Ruth, Sapphire*), and indeed in films not strictly in the cycle (e.g. the black child amidst the flames at the end of

Simba (1956); the use of children in *A Taste of Honey* (1962)). The 'unfulfilled' woman – unmarried and/or childless – is also one of the cycle's problems: *Lost* (the child is kidnapped by a spinster), *Serious Charge* (the false accusation of pederasty is brought by a spiteful spinster), *No Love for Johnnie* (Johnnie's sexless, do-gooding wife), *Victim* (Miss Benham) and the various lesbian characters. Of course, quite apart from its embeddedness in the social conscience cycle, the notion of women's only fulfilment being achieved through marriage *and* childbearing is central to the culture.

Recurrent images of childhood together with the implications of childlessness for women all suggest that not only Melville but also Laura is deviant. Not only does she choose to work with children (a classic surrogate) but she is made to choose to go on living with Melville, effectively denying both her sexuality and her childbearing potential.

Normal marriage is set up very early in the film as superior to gayness. (And indeed gayness as a real alternative lifestyle is never represented in the film.) When Barratt is on the run, he contacts his old friend Frank. The latter helps him, but his wife Sylvie is hostile. After Frank has said goodbye to Barratt, there is a bedroom scene between Frank and Sylvie. It is in fact the only scene suggesting a physical relationship in the film, and it ends with Frank telling Sylvie to be more understanding about Barratt because, 'he hasn't got what you and I have got'.

This small scene and the very important narrative fact that the Farrs stay together, have to carry the weight of the superiority of heterosexuality. For the depiction of the central heterosexual relationship depends on repression, of both their sexualities and also of her childbearing capacities. This is 'unnatural', yet the film cannot avoid it – Bogarde insisting on Melville's gayness *and* the overriding need for narrative resolution with the couple together can only be effected through repression. It is this that distorts the harmonious whole the film tried to achieve. Hence the more obvious 'failures' of the film: the way issues peter out in ambiguity, the inadequacy of Laura's role, the straining after shock effects using images of children. The challenge implicit in validating homosexuality – its assertion of sex as pleasure, its denial of procreation and monogamy as absolute needs – could not be altogether clamped down, although it would need another ten years before that challenge became organized. For this reason, then, the distortions of the repression motif do not send the whole film off course – the hegemony it is working for still largely maintains its grip.

DECODINGS

Hegemony is achieved, in so far as it is, not only in the encoding activity but also in the decoding activity. There is a tendency in discussing the moment of 'reading' either to assume one 'correct' reading or else a plethora (the familiar 'as many interpretations as there are interpreters').

Some recent work has however suggested that, while we must allow for the possibility of highly idiosyncratic variant readings, we can none the less conceptualize how something is read in terms of differences in the social situation of readers. In discussing this, I shall confine my remarks on *Victim* to the way gay people might have read it.

John Ellis in his article on Ealing studios points out that our ability to read, or decode, a text depends upon our knowledge of the codes:

> The distribution of codes necessary for the interpretation of texts is unequal: some codes are not known by almost all of the working and lower middle classes. . . . codes are not units of meaning, they are areas of connotation that are occupied differently by different classes and even class fractions, complicated by other factors such as region and sex, as well as the whole cultural experience of the viewers.
>
> (1975: 79, 80)

Gay men on the gay scene might have picked up implications in *Victim* that could have eluded others – from relatively insignificant things like recognizing the Checkers as the Salisbury, a well-known London gay pub, to something as ambiguous as the man in the bowler hat who turns out to be a policeman, whose possible job as an agent provocateur on the gay scene would probably only have occurred to people for whom police entrapment was a common hazard.

However, the way you read a film is a question not just of what your social situation is but of how you inhabit it. One cannot conclude from a person's class, gender, race, sexual orientation and so on, how she or he will read a given text (though these factors do indicate what codes she or he has access to). It is also a question of how she or he thinks and feels about living her/his social situation.

Stuart Hall in an article entitled 'Encoding/decoding' has adapted concepts from Gramsci and Frank Parkin for understanding the praxis of decoding. He suggests three types of decoding, which relate to the way a person inhabits her or his social situation – dominant, negotiated and radical. The first accepts wholesale the terms of reference of the text; that is to say, it is a reading entirely within the text's hegemonic project. The second, negotiated reading 'contains a mixture of adaptive and oppositional elements: it acknowledges the legitimacy of the hegemonic definitions to make the grand significations while, at a more restricted, situational level, it makes its own ground-rules, it operates with "exceptions" to the rule' (1980: 137). Such a reading will tend to place greater emphasis on more buried or incidental aspects of the text, although not perceiving these as contradictions to the dominant project. Finally, a radical reading develops out of the conscious, oppositional activity of a social group when it perceives itself as a political formation. Such a reading will tend to pay more attention to the contradictions in a text.

A further distinction needs to be made between negative and positive readings of the text – that is, between those that reject it (dislike it, are bored by it, disagree with it) and those that accept it (enjoy it, agree with it, feel involved with it). Whether the reading is negative or positive, the dominant/negotiated/radical distinction holds. In other words, we can describe the parameters of six types of reading.

Victim is further complicated by the fact that its overt message (that the law on homosexuality should be liberalized) and one of its covert messages (that homosexuality is a sickness) are *both* aspects of the dominant ideology concerning homosexuality in 1961. (The ideas are by no means contradictory; we have already seen this in the play upon the notion of 'nature' within *Victim*; and it is in terms of homosexuality being a relatively harmless incurable sickness that the Wolfenden Committee recommended law reform.) Negative and positive readings of *Victim* may respond to either, or both, of these messages.

Negative readings by gay people of *Victim* may be schematized as follows. Read within the terms of dominance, the film would be rejected largely on the grounds that it 'failed' (it is badly made, points are muffed, the message is obscured). The film's project remains unquestioned; only its realization faulted. In addition, one of the messages, as outlined in the previous paragraph, might be used against the other – e.g. the film is too liberal, because homosexuality is sick; or the film is not liberal enough in its depiction of homosexuality. A negotiated reading would tend to reject the film because it did not correspond with the viewer's own experience of the gay world. This would express itself in terms such as 'unrealistic', 'unconvincing', not 'the way things are', or there being 'no one in the film to identify with'. A radical rejection would object to the lack of self-determination that the liberal message implies for gay people (as witness their narrative passivity) and to the whole concept of sickness, deformity and so on built into much of the film's imagery of gayness.

A positive reading of the film would, if it was working within the dominant frame, either endorse the reformist platform of the liberal message or else, alternatively and self-oppressively, accept as true and accurate the film's imagery of sickness. A negotiated reading would find that the film did tally with the viewer's own experience, though this might be felt positively (accepting one's gayness), negatively (disliking being gay) or, most likely, ambiguously. (I suspect that a typical negotiated reading would not reject the sickness motif nor the need for law reform, but would incorporate these into the thriller elements of the film and the depiction of a gay 'bohemia' to stress the 'excitement' of gayness, a thrilled sense of belonging to an underworld.) A radical reading that was also positive about the film would see in it the delineation of oppression (e.g. blackmail, police entrapment and prejudice, contemptuous attitudes) and also a model of coming out, being open about one's gayness, both in the decision of Farr to take the blackmailers to court and in Bogarde's decision to play the role. It might also detect the element of repression in the depiction of the heterosexual marriage, although this is very buried indeed, and I doubt if I would have seen it without (a) working on the film and (b) the experience of several years' involvement with the gay movement.

To know which of these various readings predominated in the years of the film's release we would need to insert this analysis into the kind of social history of the period we do not yet have. It is possible that the gaps and fissures in the text were seized upon as foundations in the development of a resistant or even radical gay consciousness, although my own belief is that gay self-oppression was – and still is – far more widespread than we always recognize, so that *Victim*, where it was not rejected, was accepted in terms of passivity ('we can't do anything') and sickness. My final suggestion then – but it is only a suggestion – is that *Victim*'s chief social significance is that it helped gays to continue thinking of themselves in self-oppressive ways, although perhaps less harshly self-oppressive than in previous times.

Film Form 2 (1977)

NOTE

1 *Anders als die Anderen* (1919) in fact anticipates all of these. See Dyer 1990.

REFERENCES

Clarke, John, Hall, Stuart, Jefferson, Tony, and Roberts, Brian (1975) 'Subcultures, Cultures and Class', *Working Papers in Cultural Studies* 7/8 ('*Resistance Through Rituals*'): 9–74.

Dyer, Richard (1990) 'Less and More than Women and Men: Lesbian and Gay Cinema in Weimar Cinema', *New German Critique* 51: 5–60.

Ellis, John (1975) 'Made in Ealing', *Screen* 16 (1): 78–127.

Elsaesser, Thomas (1971) 'Why Hollywood?', *Monogram* 1: 4–10.

Hall, Stuart (1980) 'Encoding/decoding', in Stuart Hall, Dorothy Hobson, Andrew Lowe and Paul Willis (eds) *Culture, Media, Language*, London: Hutchinson, 128–38.

Johnston, Claire (1973) 'Women's Cinema as Counter-Cinema', in Claire Johnston (ed.) *Notes on Women's Cinema*, London: SEFT; also in Bill Nichols (ed.) *Movies and Methods*, Berkeley: University of California Press, 1976, 208–17.

Lindgren, Ernest (1948) *The Art of the Film*, London: Allen & Unwin.

Lovell, Alan and Hillier, Jim (1972) *Studies in Documentary*, London: Secker & Warburg.

Manvell, Roger (1944) *Film*, Harmondsworth: Penguin.

Perkins, V. F. (1972) *Film as Film*, Harmondsworth: Penguin.

Rotha, Paul (1948) *The Film Till Now*, London: Vision Press.

Wollen, Peter (1972) 'Counter Cinema: *Vent d'est*', *Afterimage* 4; also in Bill

Chapter 8

Male sexuality in the media

One would think that writing about images of male sexuality would be as easy as anything. We live in a world saturated with images, drenched in sexuality. But this is one of the reasons why it is in fact difficult to write about. Male sexuality is a bit like air – you breathe it in all the time, but you aren't aware of it much. Until quite recently, what was talked about was the mysterious topic of female sexuality, or else the subject of deviant male sexual practices. Ordinary male sexuality was simply sexuality, and everybody knew what it was. As I'll be arguing later, we look at the world through ideas of male sexuality. Even when not looking *at* male sexuality, we are looking at the world within its terms of reference.

Given the range and pervasiveness of imagery of male sexuality in the media, I have decided to concentrate on three specific aspects: the visual symbols for it, the treatment of it in comedy, and the way it informs the telling of stories. These aspects lie behind the very varied images of male sexuality that the media throw up – they are part of a sexual grammar that underlies and structures the vast majority of representations of male sexuality. The first and last aspects – symbols and storytelling – are so routine that they feel almost natural, just 'the way things are done'; and by their seeming so obvious and inevitable, we can lose sight of the fact that what they are actually representing is a particular sense of male sexuality, with its own history and social form. Comedy too may reproduce these seemingly natural ideas of human sexuality but it is contradictory as well, often exploding the myths of male sexuality by raising a laugh. These then are the topics I shall be covering, drawing my examples mainly from film and television but also occasionally from other visual media.

THE SYMBOLISM OF MALE SEXUALITY

Outside pornography, sexuality, male or female, is not so much shown directly as symbolized. It is not just censorship that insists on this – sexuality is on the whole better represented through symbolism. Colours, textures, objects, effects of light, the shape of things, all convey sexuality through evocation, resonance and association; they set off feelings about what sex is like more efficiently than just showing acts of sex. Pornography too uses the devices of symbolism to construct a particular sense of the sex it shows. What is significant is how sexuality is symbolized, how these devices evoke a sense of what sexuality is like, how they contribute to a particular definition of sexuality.

The first thing to say about the symbolism of male sexuality is that it is overwhelmingly centred on the genitals, especially the penis. Penises are not shown, but the evocation of male sexuality is almost always an evocation of the penis. Male sexuality is repeatedly equated with the penis; men's sexual feelings are rendered as somehow being 'in' their penises. Sexual arousal in women, where it is represented at all, may use a plethora of indications – arching bodies, undulating shoulders, hands caressing breasts, hips, arms, textures and surfaces that suggest all this – such is the vocabulary of female desire in the media. With men, the symbolism implies the erect penis. Mae West's famous gag, 'Is that a gun in your pocket or are you just pleased to see me?', characteristically goes straight to the point, that male pleasure in seeing a woman will be visibly registered in the penis, that male sexual pleasure is seen to happen in the penis. The list of objects that have been used as penis symbols is endless – trains going into tunnels, cigars raised from the lips, guns held close to the hips, and so on *ad nauseam*. However, there is no other accepted symbol of male arousal, even though we know that many zones of the male body are erogenous. Even when other parts of the male body are used to represent sexuality it is only because they can symbolize the penis, as in the commonest symbol of them all, the fist raised from the elbow.

One of the striking characteristics about penis symbols is the discrepancy between the symbols and what penises are actually like. Male genitals are fragile, squashy, delicate things; even when erect, the penis is spongy, seldom straight, and rounded at the tip, while the testicles are imperfect spheres, always vulnerable, never still. There are very exceptional cases where something of the exquisiteness and softness of the male genitals is symbolized. Constance Beeson, in her film of male gay love, uses the imagery of the flower's stamen (*Stamen* is the title of her film) to evoke the male genitals. Jean Genet, in his writings and his film, *Un Chant d'amour*, also uses flowers to symbolize the penis, and writes of an erection being like a flower unfolding. In a particularly delicate scene he uses the image of a straw pushed through a wall (in the prison where the film is set), with one man blowing smoke through it into the mouth of another – the thin, easily broken straw, the gentle wisps of smoke, these are blatant but soft images of the penis and semen in fellatio. Such imagery also suggests that male genitals can be thought of as beautiful, and there are instances of male nude painting and photography which do treat the genitals as if they are something lovely to look at – for instance, Sylvia Sleigh's gently ironic paintings, or the tradition of gay male photography that deliberately evokes classical antiquity. Yet such examples are marginal. Far more commonly the soft, vulnerable charm of male genitals is rendered as hard, tough, and dangerous. It is not flowers that most commonly symbolize male genitals but swords, knives, fists, guns.

One of the steamiest images of male sexual arousal in the cinema occurs near the beginning of the classic Japanese film *Rashomon*. The warrior, played by Toshiro Mifune, lies half-naked and unshaven under a tree. A beautiful woman passes by escorted by her husband. Mifune does not move, but his eyes stare at her off-screen, and gradually the sword that is dangling over his knee rises up at an angle to his body. A hard, gleaming weapon is at once understood to be like a penis; impossible to imagine flower imagery being used as a prelude to this tale of rape and seduction.

Yet even erect the penis and testicles are not hard, tough, weapon-like. The penis cannot stab and do all the other violent things it is evoked as being capable of, for fear of being hurt itself by doing so; even in rape, it is the humiliation, and the other actual weapons used, that do more damage than the penis itself. Moreover, the penis is also the symbol of male potency, the magic and mystery of the phallus, the endowment that appears to legitimate male power. Yet penises are only little things (even big ones) without much staying power, pretty if you can learn to see them like that, but not magical or mysterious or powerful in themselves, that is, not objectively full of real power.

Visual symbolism not only reduces male sexuality to the penis, cutting us off from other erotic pleasures, and placing on the penis a burden of being driving, tough, aggressive, it also tends to separate men from their sexuality. The penis is seen to have a life of its own, leading the man on almost despite himself. At best the man is seen as the possessor or owner of this object, but it is an object over which he does not have full control. It is the beast below.

The idea of the penis, and hence of male sexuality, as separable from the man forms the basis of stories about male sexuality, especially those with a violent or bestial view of sexual intercourse itself. Pursuit, seduction, rape, murder – not only are these different story events hard to distinguish from each other, not only do the bellicose symbols of male sexuality so easily lend themselves to the representation of sexuality as violence, but also the sense of the penis–weapon being apart from the man often absolves him of responsibility for his actions. It is not the man that is being aggressive, it is his penis. Even stories of rape and murder that do not seek to make a hero of the rapist/murderer (as many do), that present acts of rape and murder as repulsive (and not the turn-on that so many representations suggest these acts to be), that do not seek to blame women, these none the less suggest that the man can't help it – it was his *penis* that did it.

This excuse for rape really pulls together two arguments. Firstly, it does not distinguish between power/domination and sexuality; it explains male power over women in terms of sexuality, a sexuality habitually symbolized in terms of weaponry and aggressive drive. Acts of power and domination, such as rape and murder, are seen as acts of sexuality. Since sexuality is supposedly natural, acts that express it can be viewed as pre-social and irresponsible because they are beyond social or individual responsibility. Secondly, the idea of the separateness of male sexuality, 'it's all happening down there', leads to accepting the natural irresponsibility of men. What I want to stress here is the habitual seeing of male sexuality as separate, down there, apart, not a part. It may be that the given physiology of male and female genitals – men's hanging down away from the body, women's tucked up inside it – is the last resort of this argument. Women are somehow connected to their sexuality in a way that men are not. We don't have to make sense of our different sexualities in this way, but the given visible difference has certainly suited patriarchial arguments that men 'can't help' having bestial desires.

The most common imagery of male sexuality, then, focuses on the penis as the locus of male sexuality, and sees the penis in a particular way – down there, hard, importunate. This is an extraordinarily constricted and ugly way of imagining the erotic, which makes it difficult to portray male sexual experience in terms of tenderness and beauty. It is also very tough, serious and po-faced, which is why you can't help wanting to giggle at it some-times, and why it is such a rich source of comedy.

COMEDY

Sex comedy is one of the artistic forms (horror stories are another) that consistently plays on ambivalences surrounding male sexuality, some of them stemming from the symbolism I've just been discussing. Comedy is an area of expression that is licensed to explore aspects of life that are difficult, contradictory and distressing. I don't mean to imply that comedy is inherently subversive but simply to suggest that comedy can get away with making fun of things that other genres with a more straight-faced attitude cannot. Popular comedy tends particularly to exploit the contra-dictory nature of things, of attitudes, precisely because it aims to be popular, to appeal to different people with different attitudes. If a gag or a sketch can gather together these different contradictory attitudes it will be more popular, if only in the numerical sense of appealing to more people.

Comedy is then fertile terrain for considering images of sexuality. I want to look here at explicit, even crude, sex comedy: seaside postcards, *Carry On* films, the American sex comedies of the 1950s and 1960s (for instance, *The Seven Year Itch, The Girl Can't Help It, Pillow Talk*), television sitcoms such as *George and Mildred, Are You Being Served?* and *Hi-De-Hi!*, and comedians such as Frankie Howerd and Benny Hill. Much of this humour plays on the anxiety caused by the gap between what male genitals are actually like and what they are supposed to be like. Humour can touch on male fears about the inability to live up to what penises claim for them and can endorse female derision about the patriarchial overestimation of the penis.

There is, for instance, a seaside postcard which shows (from behind) a muscleman holding a barbell aloft; he is surrounded by kneeling, bikini-clad, nubile women; his trunks have slipped off round his thighs. The gag line is 'It's magnificent, but he can't keep it up for five minutes'. All the women are staring fixedly at the man's penis; the expressions on their faces flatter male estimation of the effect the sight of male genitals has on women, namely awe and delight. However, the man's expression is not of sexual pride but of embarrassment at having been revealed; his is the standard male face in seaside postcards, bright red, snub-nosed, a face normally associated with the hen-pecked, feckless male. And the gag line greatly deflates male pride, hitting on one of the great male fears about penetration and sex, that of not being able to keep it going, not staying hard.

Much sexual comedy plays on the idea of the penis apart from the man, leading him on into mischief, making a fool of him. Such comedy can both ridicule men, subject them to indignities, and yet also validate the idea of male sexuality as essentially asocial, outside of social construction and responsibility. The British comedy film *Percy* deals with a shy man who, as a result of an accident, has to have a penis transplant; the donor is a randy womanizer. With this new penis, Percy finds that, despite his modest reserve, he is constantly running after women, led on by his genitals. His penis doesn't belong to him, it is importunate, he can't help himself. It's a sharp comic idea, although in the event a dreary movie.

The apparent butt of sexual comedy is often a woman – yet, as so often with images of women, the joke is often really about men. Two female types are particularly common – the harridan and the busty blonde. The first symbolizes male hostility to women; the latter on the other hand seems primarily concerned with exposing male weakness.

Among the more familiar incarnations of the harridan are the fat women from comic postcards, the dame in pantomime, and more recently, Mildred in the television comedy *George and Mildred*. We are asked to laugh at her on three accounts. Firstly there is simply the fact that she is ugly – mounds of flesh for the postcard woman; excessive, strident makeup and hair-dos for the dame; and for Mildred, the cruel distortion of Yootha Joyce's portrayal. Then secondly, despite being ugly, she offers herself as attractive – the tiny polka-dot hat atop the fat woman of the postcards; the brilliant colours, elaborate gowns and peekaboo underclothes of the dame; Mildred's bright hair-dye and even brighter lipstick. So, we are to laugh because they are not attractive, and then because they come on as if they are. A quintessential scene that brings these two elements together is the trying on of the slipper in any production of *Cinderella*, where the Ugly Sisters (as they are unabashedly called) primp up their stick-out bosoms, pucker their wildly misshapen lips and flutter their outrageously enormous eyelashes at a condescendingly amused Prince Charming. All the pretences of presentation that society wishes on women are here seen as coming from women as self-deceiving narcissism, all the more vicious, in *Cinderella*, for being practised at the expense of a poor, innocent – and, of course, beautiful – young girl. We can turn this comedy inside out and see that it expresses male resentment at finding women sexually arousing, male jealousy that it is women who are allowed to present themselves with such allure. Yet this tradition of humour never says as much. We have to bring such a view from outside the humour.

There is a third, related reason why the harridan is supposed to be funny, and that is because she's randy and predatory. The whole gag about Mildred is that she wanted sex, a want that poor little George could not satisfy. Harridans do not have to be grotesque to be funny; it is enough for them to be sexually alert. Ruth Madoc in *Hi-De-Hi!* is neat, pretty and smart, yet her constant desire for men makes her a comic terror. Here again we can see comedy working its magic, turning terror into laughter; but we have to work harder to see that this comic image expresses male fears and anxieties about female sexual energy, about the way it may test virility, about the way it challenges male supremacy.

Comedy that uses the image of the nubile, large-bosomed blonde woman only in part laughs at this figure of fun. Jayne Mansfield, Barbara Windsor and the string of performers featured in Benny Hill's shows are often at the centre of gags concerned with the extraordinary impact on men of overwhelming, uncontrollable sexual arousal. When Mansfield walks down the street in *The Girl Can't Help It*, a man unloading a huge block of ice finds it turning to steam in his hands – her impact just turns him red hot. The image that most immediately evokes British farce is a man with his trousers round his ankles wearing undershorts with brightly coloured, silly motifs upon them. The narrative that has led to this is nearly always the man's inability to stop himself, to stop his penis, from running after 'girls'. Benny Hill's whole act is a constant state of gleeful arousal – he is the man from the seaside postcard personified, round-faced, red-cheeked, snub-nosed. His clothes are always foolish, they never enhance or dignify his body but coarsen and vulgarize it. And he spends all his time ogling or chasing women, no matter what he is supposed to be doing. Many sketches are simply built around him starting off doing something and being instantly, ineluctably, catastrophically, but delightedly distracted by a bouncily-bosomed blonde woman passing by. Benny Hill in pursuit of women is never anything other than foolish to look at, and this is often accompanied by visual gags where paint brushes, lollipops or whatever are used as symbols of the eager and ridiculous penis.

Such perpetual randiness (of the little man in the seaside postcards, or Benny Hill, or George Formby or Sid James) robs men of any claim to be taken seriously but also embraces grotty physicality as the stuff of life. It was in terms like these that George Orwell defended the seaside postcard in his article (1961) on the postcard artist, Donald McGill. Orwell suggested that postcard humour is an acknowledgement that life is not ideal, that sexual dreams and fantasies are only part of our makeup, that we also all know life to be mucky, awkward and scrappy, that sex especially is tacky. The image of male sexuality in postcards and comedy films is a welcome acceptance and embrace of the shortcomings of life, and Orwell is right to suggest that comedy can teach us a kind of robust, cheery recognition that sex (and all other facets of physical existence) falls far short of our ideals. Yet there are problems with this view of human sexual frailty. It celebrates sexual grottiness as if it were a permanent feature of the human condition; it promotes acceptance of male sexual failure in concert with derogatory and spiteful views of female sexuality; and its own itchy, tetchy squeamishness is itself a product of a society which loathes the human body.

Comedy is unruly – it can no more be secured for the right-on than it can for the right-wing. In comedy we see now a reinforcement of ideas expressed by the imagery of male sexuality, and now an undermining of them. What there isn't (at least, I can't think of an example) is comedy which shows that male sexuality need not be importunate, uncontrollable and quickly exhausted. Most comedy does in the end insist that, no matter how absurd male sexuality may be, that is what it is like. Comedy may often undermine men by ridiculing their sexuality but it still ends up asserting as natural the prevalent social definition of that sexuality.

MALE SEXUAL NARRATIVE

So far I've been concentrating on how male sexuality is represented through male characters, performers and visual imagery. But the most insistent and relentless representation of male sexuality is not in how men are represented at all, but rather in the way that women are looked at by the camera eye. The very basic methods that film and television have developed for telling stories imply a particular sense of what male sexuality is. I am not talking here of the way that films centre on male protagonists whom we are all invited to identify with, and whose (generally sexist) attitudes to women we are supposed to share – though this is certainly a major feature of most media stories. Nor am I considering the way that narratives are structured around sexuality as pursuit, the man chasing the woman, that type of narrative that elides love, seduction, possession and rape. What I want to focus on here is the formal organization of storytelling

– any story, not just an overtly sexual one – that reinforces a notion of male sexuality. I'll end by talking about the overall structure of narratives, but I'd like first to look at the way that we are invited to enter the fictional world of the story from scene to scene so as to see things from the male point of view, and moreover to see things through a particular sexual sensibility, that of the dominant notion of male sexuality. Much of the pleasure on offer depends on our experience of all kinds of sequences through this male sexuality. I want here to describe and discuss two of the most standard sequences in popular entertainment film and television – the 'heroine in jeopardy' sequence and the 'lovers' first meeting' scene.

First, the heroine in jeopardy. In a horror film she has perhaps left her bedroom at night because she's heard a noise, she goes wandering through the twisting corridors of the gothic mansion anxiously holding aloft her guttering candle. In a thriller, she's perhaps gone visiting in a block of flats, one which happens to hide a psychopath on the run. The person she's gone to visit isn't there, and there's no one else around; she can't seem to open the front door and doesn't know what to do when the psychopath hears her rattling at the door. Or in a science fiction series, peak time *Dr Who* for instance, everyone is running to get away from the monster, whatever it is, and the heroine trips; she catches her ankle and the monster gets nearer. In all these cases it is always a woman who is trapped, a woman without resources to help herself. Heroes in jeopardy do something about it; heroines don't. And the pleasure we are supposed to get from seeing these sequences is that of seeing a woman in peril. We're supposed to get off on her vulnerability, her hysteria, her terror. In the way such sequences are put together, we are encouraged to take up a traditional male role in relation to the woman, one that asserts our superiority and at the same time encourages us to feel the desire to rape and conquer. We are superior because we either know more than her (we know that psychopath is there but she hasn't spotted him yet), or because we can see what any sensible person would do but she, foolishly and pathetically, doesn't.

We are encouraged into the position of a rapist in relation to her. For one thing, we can see her but she can't see us – this is true of all film and television characters, obviously enough, but it is really played on here because it gets the female character into situations where, if she knew she could be seen, she'd be on her guard, she'd protect her body symbolically from our gaze with gestures and clothes. As it is however, the gothic heroine's nightgown is inadequately buttoned up so that her bosom glows in the candlelight; the escaping heroine who's caught her leg in something wriggles to get free and her skirt rides higher and higher up her thigh. Exposing the body makes flesh available to the gaze of whoever is around. Female flesh is thought to provoke the heterosexual male viewer; the sight of it can make him want to take it – the sight of it exposed by a woman in a vulnerable situation who is doubly vulnerable because she, as a character, doesn't know we're sitting there in the dark watching. This puts us in the classic rapist-watching-in-the-shadows position. Sometimes, quite often in fact, we are even more explicitly put in the rapist's position. We see the heroine from the point of view of the lurking fiend, psychopath or monster. One of the commonest climactic camera shots in sequences like this has the heroine backing away from the camera, looking at it in terror, cringing in helplessness. She is looking at us; we are the raging fiend.

But she is rescued by the hero, who is our stand-in, our identification figure. The camera puts us in the position of the rapist, but the plot puts us reassuringly back in the position of the saviour. This once again establishes our superiority – she needed the man/us to come to her rescue, she'll now be in our debt, subordinate to our masterful actions. (If this is none too edifying for the male audience, heaven knows what it does for women in the audience.)

The stock-in-trade of popular film and television is the pleasure of thrills, terror and horror, and there is nothing inherently objectionable in this. What is at issue is the way these pleasures are time and time again set up for us in ways that equate the general excitement of suspense and tension with sexual excitement, power over women, the thrill of taking a woman and the reassurance of female subordination. In such sequences we are not so much shown men or men's sexuality as invited to see and feel it. We are invited to place ourselves in relation to women as heterosexual men, easily and uncontrollably aroused by the sight of women, heady in power over the weak.

A second commonplace sequence also asks us to identify with hetero-sexual feelings, to agree with its idea of what heterosexual male feelings are; it also encourages us to go on believing such feelings exist. This sequence shows the moment when the hero first sees the heroine, when he looks at her with love or desire. It goes something like this: shot of hero looking at something off camera, he lit in standard lighting; long held shot of heroine looking down or away, not at the hero, lit in soft glow, glamour lighting; back to shot of him looking at her. The conventions of matching shots make it absolutely clear that he is looking at her but she doesn't know that he is. Sometimes, towards the end of the shot she will look in his direction, but only momentarily; then she will avert her eyes. As Nancy Henley shows in her book *Body Politics* (1977), this reproduces the convention of looks and glances in actual heterosexual exchanges. Men stare at women, women submit to being looked at, or at most steal a glance.

The fact that the woman often doesn't know she is being looked at once again makes her vulnerable. And, once again, we are invited to relate to the heroine through this version of heterosexual male sexuality. We don't see male arousal, the hero seldom speaks or expresses his feelings, there is no exploration of those feelings from the outside – all there is an encouragement to experience male sexuality in the act of looking, looking at the screen, looking at women.

I've been describing two very commonplace sequences. Many have argued that the devices used, the way the camera places us as voyeur, the way editing puts us into the position of the male, the way the narrative encourages us to identify with the man, compose the very basic storytelling grammar of mainstream film and television fiction. The argument can be taken further to suggest that virtually all narratives, regardless of what medium they are in, reproduce the way male sexuality is organized, to the extent that it is hard to tell whether narrative structure is based on how we think of male sexuality or whether our conception of male sexuality is derived from the pleasures of male dominance within narratives.

There is a suggestive similarity in the way both male sexuality and narrative are commonly described. Male sexuality is said to be goal-oriented; seduction and foreplay are merely the means by which one gets to the 'real thing', an orgasm, the great single climax. Equally, it has been suggested that if one compares the underlying structure of most narratives in Western fiction, it is about the pursuit of a goal and its attainment, usually through possession. Thus male sexuality is like a story, or stories are like male sexuality. Both keep women in their place.

Since men are the central protagonists of all but a few specifically feminine narrative genres (for instance, romance) and are also the ones given the active roles as the characters who make things happen and who move the narrative along, women function either as the goal of the narrative or as the reward for achieving that goal. In this way, narratives reproduce the connection with sexuality. Even if the narrative appears to be about war, crime, business or whatever, the drive to a climax is so bound up with the promise of a woman at the end that all stories seem to be modelled on male sexuality. It is no accident that the word climax applies to orgasm and narrative. In both, the climax is at once what sex and story aim at and also the signal that the sex and the story are over. The placing of the women and the men in stories ensures that a heterosexual model is reasserted, in which women represent what male sexuality is ostensibly there for. Women are the goal or the reward, they are the occasion of male sexuality – and yet they play no active part in it. The man drives himself, or his penis drives him; it is he who 'reaches' the climax.

Are all narratives like this? Must they be? What I've described is an overall *tendency* in twentieth-century media fiction; it is economical, dynamic, efficient, finished – qualities we are brought up to respect and qualities which, as *part of* the spectrum of human qualities, have much to commend them. But it is by no means only in elite and experimental fiction that we can find something else. The complex frustrations of film noir narrative, the unending multiple climaxes of soap opera, the way song numbers in most musicals interrupt narrative flow as expressions of mutual delight between people, the episodic structure of many comedies and some adventure stories, which dispense with the idea of a goal as such – all these suggest that there is room for manoeuvre, not only in terms of woman-centred narratives but also in terms of stories centred on either sex that are not told and felt through the eyes of an oppressive male sexuality.

One would not and should not expect a society run in the interests of men to produce too many images that go against this. The visual representation of male sexuality puts women in their place, as objects of a 'natural' male sexual drive that may at times be ridiculous but is also insistent, inescapable and inevitable. Such representations help to preserve the existing power relations of men over women by translating them into sexual relations, rendered both as biologically given and as a source of masculine pleasure. What is perhaps more surprising is that these images should, by and large, be so unattractive, so straight and narrow, so dreary. Men too are fixed in place by this imagery, and if theirs is a place of superiority it is none the less a cramped, sordid, compulsive little place with its hard-edged contours and one-off climaxes.

No society is unified and homogenous. If it were, change could not be imagined, there could be no images of something else. There are other images of male sexuality – in some gay and feminist art, which is where you'd hope to find it, and also within the mainstream, popular (but largely unrespectable) traditions of comedy and romance. Here and there we do get a vision of a sexuality that is not nasty and brutish, silly and pathetic, but varied, sensuous, langorous, warm and welcome. We need to see it more often in order to live it more fully.

From Martin Humphries and Andy Metcalf (eds) *The Sexuality of Men*, London: Pluto (1985)

REFERENCES

Henley, Nancy M. (1977) *Body Politics*, New York: Prentice-Hall.
Orwell, George (1961) 'The Art of Donald McGill', in *Collected Essays*, London: Secker & Warburg, 167–78. (First published in 1942.)

FURTHER READING

Cameron, Deborah and Frazer, Elizabeth (1987) *The Lust to Kill*, Cambridge: Polity Press.
Holloway, Wendy (1984) 'Gender Differences and the Production of Subjectivity', in Julian Henriques *et al.* (eds) *Changing the Subject*, London: Methuen, 227–63.
Lehman, Peter (1988) '*In the Realm of the Senses*: Desire, Power, and the Representation of the Male Body', *Genders* 2: 91–110.
Mercer, Kobena and Julien, Isaac (1988) 'Race, Sexual Politics and Black

Chapter 9

Brief affairs

Personally I'm pleased that the little chap in the new Levi's ad is wearing sparkling white, generously cut briefs. If it does for them what the launderette version did for boxer shorts, I'll be well content. This, I might add, has nothing whatsoever to do with personal taste, but does also suggest a shift in attitudes towards the male body that is some advance on the usual mix of disdain, derision or misplaced awe.

The Levi's ad is not an isolated event. For some time now, the image of men's underwear has been, so to speak, coming out of the closet. Designer labels – Armani, Cerruti, Calvin Klein – have been bringing out their own lines and there's been a retro cult for Y-fronts and Fruit of the Loom that has made even these labels seem designer orientated.

Nikos – whose new boutique opened in London in 1989 – is really known only for his underwear. In France, Italy and some other European countries, boutiques specializing in underwear, either men's or men's and women's, are now quite common. Nor is this just a phenomenon of haute couture – British Home Stores, Burtons, Top Man, Next and other high street chains now offer a range of underwear clearly emulating Nikos *et al.* It's all very different from how we used to think and feel about how to cover up what's down there.

Men's knickers have generally been perceived in two modes. One is medical – all those considerations about the healthiness of hanging free versus support – a set of views that, significantly, only ever aroused controversy when it was suggested that tight briefs might lead to impotence. The other is giggling, which is in part an admirable response to seeing men divested of the dignity of trousers, but which also suggests that there must be something intrinsically silly about what men wear under their trousers.

That point has been further rubbed home by countless wags' penchants for ill-cut shorts in polka-dot, hearts and cupid designs, or seaside gift shops offering miscoloured nylon briefs with leering snakes or tadpoles adorning the relevant parts. It's the stupidity of male sexual desire that is at stake here, splendidly cut down to size, but correspondingly naturalized as silly.

The revival of boxer shorts was a (hopefully) last ditch attempt to keep those modes in circulation. Though beige and fetchingly buttock hugging on Nick Kamen, and available in the designer labels in plain colours or simple patterns, boxers rapidly became the vehicle of the old silly motifs and slogans in all those tube and rail outlets. Certainly a garment that doesn't cling to the body is likely to be less grubby when it comes to washday and will make less explicit that part of the male body too often associated with boredom, obligation or rape. Is it easier to work up some sexual enthusiasm for men's sexual parts when the latters' association with drudgery, dreariness and violence is played down? As long as women still have a servicing relationship to men's clothes and bodies, other percep-tions of men's underwear may seem to fall wide of the mark – however, these perceptions might be worth examining if they could suggest other forms of relationship.

There always was another way of perceiving men's underwear of course, to be found in the pages of gay magazines and scores of mail order catalogues offered, with varying degrees of explicitness, to the gay market. Bikini briefs were the greatest success, mass marketed as 'skants' by the 1960s and becoming a staple of men's underwear ever since. They were overtly 'sexy' yet, partly because of their gay association, perhaps slightly overdid it. The emphasis on smallness had an uneasy relation with obses-sive concerns about bigness, and their name and style recalled women's underwear, fine for the androgynous 1960s but less so for the difference-loving 1980s. In short, if there was to be a revision in men's underwear, that was not where it would draw its inspiration.

The new men's underwear, which like practically all male fashion was also pioneered by gay men, draws on two earlier styles, often simul-taneously.

On the one hand, the new designs often use the wide waist bands and sharply cut away pouch of the jock strap – most obvious in many of Nikos's briefs, which are the ironic culmination of a gay sartorial history. The jock strap was the image of straight masculinity, a purely functional garment associated with the, then, macho world of sport. It became a talisman of desire in much gay pornography, associated with the men you could not, but then just might, have. Throughout the 1970s, how-ever, what had been objects of desire, associated with the status of straightness, were taken over by gay male culture. Gay men increasingly turned themselves into their own objects of desire – hence working out, 501s and jock straps. In Nikos's versions, function is blatantly irrelevant, everything is exaggerated (more cut away, thicker waist bands), sexiness is all.

The other source for the new underwear is the jockey brief aka Y-fronts. Their introduction was a key moment in the history of men's underwear. It is the bra of that history. Like the latter, it moulds the body part concerned into a streamlined form, an attractive and inaccurate bulge. This bit of the male anatomy allows a little more room for manoeuvre than the female breast, leading to the distinction, immortalized for me in the words of an assistant at Marshall and Snellgrove in Birmingham in the 1960s, between men who are 'up-wearers' and those who are 'down-wearers'.

But like the bra, and even more insistently, as befitted a masculine garment in the mid-twentieth century, jockey briefs could also be passed off as practical. They offered support (something neither breasts nor testicles knew they needed) but at the same time through the frontal opening made allowance for the male genitals' other principal function. All of this made it look and feel sexy while appearing sensibly, masculinely utilitarian.

The new men's underwear, when it is not a straightforward recycling of jockey briefs, is often a postmodern collage of them and the jock strap, taking bits from one and bits from the other – wide waist bands, but full briefs; 'good' cotton with jock strap elastic; cut-away fronts but generously cut backs; and so on. Most fascinating, and postmodern, of all is the reference to the jockey brief's frontal opening. Y-fronts were always a contraption really. If the opening was cut generously enough to permit ease of use, the penis was likely to flop out of it at any time; but if it was cut small enough to prevent this, it was a bit of a fiddle pulling the penis through and then, inadequately shaken, back. Whether in acknowledgement of this perhaps insurmountable design problem, the new underwear often dispenses with frontal opening but retains the piping and stitching of the old jockey, so that it looks like there's an opening there. What once had a function – physiologically and psychologically, to make men feel all right about wearing so sensuous a garment – is now simply reduced to a decoration, a gesture at the idea of the masculine as the functional.

All of this makes the new men's underwear playfully sexy. It clearly signals sexual difference, creating explicitly erotic underwear without recourse to the feminine or androgynous. It draws on earlier versions of what might be the indelibly male in underwear, but by ingeniously recombining, eroticizing and exaggerating them it undermines the grim authority they were supposed to have. It turns humour and irony into adjuncts to, not deflaters of, sexiness.

New Statesman and Society (March 1989)

Chapter 10

Papillon

In its marketing, *Papillon* (1973) is a characteristic 1970s film. It is an event movie, with separate performances, huge tie-in publicity, blockbuster length. It is based on an enormously successful book (like *Jaws* and *The Godfather*, though with less direct relation between the production of the book and that of the film) and is built around two major male stars, hence it is also a buddy movie like *Butch Cassidy and the Sundance Kid* and *Thunderbolt and Lightfoot* and many others. Yet *Papillon* does not really deliver what its marketing promises. It drastically alters the tone of the central relationship as usually encountered in the buddy movie. For a big entertainment movie it is strikingly suffused by a melancholy regret for the impossibility of heroism, rather than sharing the 1970s tendency to send heroism up.

PAPILLON AS BUDDY MOVIE

The buddy movie presented a male–male relationship that was composed of humour, tacit understanding and, usually, equality of toughness between men. This relationship was constructed by a disavowal of the very thing that would appear to bind the men together – love. The elements that compose the relationship actually effect this disavowal – badinage as a way of not expressing serious emotions, silent communication as a means for not articulating or confronting feelings, toughness as a sign that one is above tenderness. In the relationship between Papillon (Steve McQueen) and Dega (Dustin Hoffman), *Papillon* retains some of these elements, in particular the use of humour, mostly of the dry verbal kind but occasionally slapstick, as in the episode with the crocodile. Yet for the most part, *Papillon* acknowledges that what it is treating is a love relationship. It does this partly by signifying the relationship in small but emotionally loaded details (e.g. the coconuts Dega sends to Papillon in solitary), partly through the use of the cinematic conventions for the representation of love (e.g. a direct cut from Dega's face full of fond emotion to a shot over his shoulder at Papillon lying asleep in bed). Part of the representation includes a direct recognition of the buddy movie's conventional disavowal in the fact that these men cannot actually say what they feel. This is most moving when Papillon and Dega meet after Papillon's second period in solitary – both are now prematurely old men living on a remote island. When Dega actually speaks to Papillon, having spied at him from behind bushes, he says, 'I wish you hadn't come here' in a way that indicates that Papillon's presence churns him up emotionally, and then he makes the domestic gesture, 'Are you fond of fish?' which is the cue for the music to swell in with the Papillon theme, at last fully stated (more on the music later). This treatment is reminiscent of the English treatment of passion – *Brief Encounter, Ryan's Daughter, Yanks* – where oblique statements and music betray what social conventions cannot allow to be spoken. Such a procedure is appropriate to another form of unspeakable love, that between two men.

A further feature of the buddy movie's representation of male–male relationships is its explicit denial of homosexuality. Actual sexual intercourse is performed – as a generic necessity – by each of the men separately with a woman, whose only role in the film is often that of providing the men with a screw. Gay characters are often included, usually in a grotesquely caricatured form, to signal the difference between the central buddy relationship and a homosexual one. This has been interpreted by many critics as a smokescreen, a brutal (in relation to the women characters) and hysterical (in relation to the gay characters) disavowal of the sexuality of the central relationship. This may be so, but it is a point that can be made too quickly and tends to conflate love and sexuality too readily: it does not allow for the possibility of non-sexual love. *Papillon*, though in some ways reproducing this aspect of the buddy movie, is also crucially different.

The heterosexuality of both Dega and Papillon is established for us early on, before they meet, in two moments in the march through the town (on the way to the ship bound for the penal colony) where a (different) woman signals her past relationship with each of them. Papillon's heterosexuality is further affirmed in the romantic idyll in the native village during his long escape. True to buddy movie form, these women have no function other than to signal the men's heterosexuality, and this is especially true of the native idyll with its Gauguinesque – nubile, soft mannered, bare breasted, sexually free, sweetly beautiful, unspeaking – girl devoted to serving Papillon's every need. Equally, the gay characters, Maturette and his slobbish admirer in the hospital, in part function as a model for what Papillon and Dega's relationship is *not*. But what marks the difference from the conventional buddy movie is the treatment of these characters, especially Maturette.

Maturette is granted a legitimacy in the film's adventure narrative. He is crucial in effecting the central escape, not only in distracting his admirer, the prisoner-guard, so that Papillon can knock him out but also in setting

Dega's broken leg, treating his gangrene, steering the boat and so on. As he points out to Papillon, he is also the 'toughest' of them, since he has actually killed a man. Not only does he participate fully and equally in the escape with the straight characters, he and his admirer are both presented through imagery drawn directly and vividly from gay culture, specifically from the work of Jean Genet. Physically, they resemble two types consistently evoked by Genet in his description of prisoners – Maturette, lean, athletic, pretty, his shorn hair exposing his clean shaven face, making it look vulnerable even while he is defiant; his admirer, big, uncouth, domineering, his unshaven face and gross lips a parody of masculinity. The briefly shown 'relationship' between them also reworks Genet's sexual imagery – the grotesque knife-as-phallus and, most evocatively, the flower-as-phallus, stuffed into Maturette's mouth in their first scene together. Gay men are thus granted a legitimacy, both as participants in the main adventure and in terms of the specificity of their own sub-culture. Dignity and distinctions within the latter are also asserted, notably in Maturette's hissed words in Papillon's ears, when he is shaving him and when Papillon is asking him to show the guard 'a good time' – 'You think I'm a whore, don't you? Well, you're wrong.'

Such sensitive treatment of homosexuality hardly suggests hysterical rejection of it – yet it is quite clear that Maturette is different from Papillon and Dega. When Papillon holds Dega while Maturette cuts out Dega's gangrene, there is a cut from Papillon cradling Dega in his arms to Maturette looking on, excluded from their intimacy. The love between Papillon and Dega is physical and tender, but not sexual – and this is not a rejection on the film's part of homosexuality but rather an openness to the possibility of real love between men who are none the less heterosexual. The film is thus closer to the concerns of men's liberation or men against sexism than either the gay movement or the women's movement. This is important – the beauty of non-sexual love between persons of the same sex needs representing, though, like the men's liberation movement in some of its manifestations, it does at times seem to depend on the exclusion of women. None the less, it is remarkable for a Hollywood film to represent non-sexual love between males *as love* without a concomitant hysterical rejection of homosexuality. (There is a sense in which all relationships between human individuals are in some degree 'sexual', but it seems useful to call a relationship sexual only when the sexual element is significant and defining.)

The treatment includes a certain sensuousness in the photographing of Steve McQueen – but this is not uncommon in buddy movies (especially in the lighting of Robert Redford in *Butch Cassidy and the Sundance Kid*). He is differentiated from the other men, including Dega/Hoffmann, in this respect, and hence he is made 'special'. When the others are sprayed from a hose in the hold during the voyage to Devil's Island, Papillon/McQueen stands at the back, his chest and face in warm, chiaroscuro lighting to mould his features. When the other men stand in line for food on deck, McQueen/Papillon is shot lying out sunbathing, like a *Playgirl* centrefold. He is the eponymous here, special and, for a while, he is glamorized. Yet although he remains special, this glamorization is reduced as the film proceeds. Papillon becomes, at the level of plot, more special, but the treatment cuts his specialness – his heroic status – down to size.

PAPILLON AS EPIC

The film's colour is dominated by blue, but there is a shift from a dirty grey-blue at the beginning of the film to a lusher green-blue by the end. This corresponds with a shift in the film's perspective that effectively constitutes a sort of meditation on the possibility of the heroic, and of the epic as heroism's aesthetic form, in modern times. It is in this dimension that the film clearly belongs to the work of Franklin Schaffner, one of the few directors to work consistently in the epic genre and yet in whose work there is a perceptible distance from the glorious aspirations of epic. He has tried to rework the epic in near-contemporary situations, and yet his films never quite establish the simple nobility and conviction of the traditional epic. Aside from *The War Lord*, a film that (as I dimly recall) tries to tell a feudal story in terms of the feudal value system (though not in terms of that value system as embodied in the medieval epic), Schaffner's films are almost glum in their failure to realize the epic ideal. *Nicholas and Alexandra* portrays the royal lovers as weak people caught up in events, and spends the last hour lingering over their icy demise; *Patton* is constantly drawing ironic attention to Patton's own delusions of epic status, with shots of him against the monumental ruins of past glories and with a script (by Francis Ford Coppola) in which Patton compares his strategy with that of the greats; *Planet of the Apes*, ostensibly asserting the superiority of humankind to the ape civilization, undermines this in its final shot, revealing that we are not on another planet at all but in the defeated ruins of our own. Schaffner's films retain the movie epic features – the high adventure, the conspicuously spent budget, wide screen and symphonic music, and clear cut characterizations. These ingredients usually (among exceptions, I would propose *Alexander Nevsky*, *The 300 Spartans*, *Spartacus* and *El Cid*) either work out thin and disappointing or need discussing in the different, and wholly legitimate, context of spectacle. With Schaffner, a sense is built in of the impossibility of really making an epic, a feeling, perhaps, that, for all its glories, it is an inappropriate genre for our time. It is, after all, a product of societies in which might is determined through personal strength in warfare, not through technological efficiency, ideological struggle or the accumulation of wealth through the organization of labour. The problem is that those latter forms of power lack gloriousness in our eyes and any attempt to convey such a quality now has either to be nostalgic or to be placed within the optimism (real or forced) of a new society – hence the link between socialist realism and epic. Schaffner's films do neither, but rather acknowledge the problem even while they evoke the glory.

Of none of his films is this more true than of *Papillon*. Its protagonist, as I've suggested, is treated as special – yet the quality of his specialness, especially as this might make him a true epic hero, is severely qualified, partly by what this specialness is shown to consist of and partly by the actual treatment of the sequences of epic action, the escapes.

Papillon's specialness is simply that he survives. As Northrop Frye has observed, the epic hero is different in degree but not in kind from other persons, and this is true of Papillon, but only in the sense that he stays alive in the face of appalling conditions and without resort to Dega's manipulation of corruption. His repeated shout, 'I'm still here, you bastards', encapsulates the limits of his heroism, endurance. He does not perform great deeds – rather, his heroism is focused on the most inglorious images. His first words in the film draw attention to the habit of all the prisoners of hiding their belongings up their arses; a turning point in the second escape is his encounter with the leper colony; and the film dwells on images of crabs, cockroaches, bats and centipedes, the environment of his heroism. The big moments of courage are shaking a leper's hand and eating a centipede.

There are more expansive actions (a defining quality of the epic), notably the second escape leading to the seaside idyll and the final escape on the raft of coconuts. Yet the treatment of these undercuts their expansiveness. With the first, there is a rapid escalation of the fantastic. After the classic epic shots of the raft on the high seas against the horizon, and after Dega and Maturette have been captured, Papillon takes flight into the mythic. His companion, initially, is a Che Guevara look-alike, evoking a contemporary legend; a spectacular long shot shows them running up the steps of an ancient ruin, perhaps an Aztec or Incan fortress; they run through a bizarre, other-worldly landscape of what looks like upturned tree stumps bleached by the sun into twisted, gnarled shapes; they are chased by Indians with blow-pipes. And then, with another moment of spectacle, Papillon's leap in slow motion into a pool with a huge waterfall, we suddenly cut, in a transition never to be explained, to the native seaside village and the softly sexist and racist idyll that follows. The more heroic, in a traditional sense, Papillon becomes, the more the film ironically undercuts his actions, by casting them in the language of myth, moving away from the naturalistic style of the early part of the film.

The final escape is treated differently and, given that it is the last and successful escape, almost perfunctorily. Far more time is spent on the lovingly cantankerous relationship between Papillon and Dega than on the escape. And the final shot of the film (before the long credits sequence, that is) is a striking denial of the standard heroic last shot. Papillon struggles aboard his coconut raft and the camera begins to pan upwards. We expect a final shot of him paddling off to the horizon, the hero making his destiny. Instead we get a cut to a skimming aerial shot, so that we see Papillon from above, spread-eagled on his raft, shouting 'I'm still here, you bastards'. The camera then zooms slowly back, flattening out the image, and leaving Papillon pinned down on the churning blue sea that fills out the scope screen. There is no sense of his going anywhere. We leave him there, not reaching safety and freedom, though a voice-over tells us that that is what happens.

This final shot is accompanied by the most full-bodied statement of the Papillon theme in the film. The gradual introduction of this theme into the film underscores the film's general movement from a bleak depiction of misery to an ironic treatment of epic. As a tune, it resembles the stereotype of French popular music (I recently heard it placed, accurately enough, on a Muzak tape of 'French' melodies). The film is sparing in its use. There is, anyway, no music for the first quarter of an hour or so, which is all hard, unemotional, naturalistic narrative. The first use of music accompanies the arrival at Devil's Island, and contains hints of the Papillon theme but lost beneath an *agitato* violin melody and visuals of a convict being shot and a woman chopping the head off a huge fish. As the film proceeds – and moves towards the mythic – the tune is more completely stated, notably over the raft voyage in the second escape, but it is only fully used in the last sequence – firstly to underscore the sentiment of Papillon and Dega's relationship and then, most triumphantly, over the final, pre-credits shots. Here it is played, against full orchestra, by that most media-archetypal of French instruments, the accordion. The more the theme is confidently played, and the more cod Frenchness is emphasized, the more ironically mythic the film becomes. The elation of the final moments, albeit moderated by irony, is then cut short as the credits run over the ruins of Devil's Island, accompanied by a deeply gloomy score.

The original book is surrounded by much speculation as to its authenticity, and the film no doubt takes it cue from this for its ambiguous treatment of the hero and his deeds (further emphasized by condensing the thirteen escapes of the book into the three of the film). There is also a thread of details that counterpoint the dream of heroism with the reality of money. Although this is clearly not what most interests the film, there is a definite sense of Papillon being caught up in a system based on money. This is Dega's view – he is constantly referring to things in terms of money, and plays the system (both the stockmarket and the penal colony) in terms of subterfuge and bribery. For him, the realization that Papillon has risked his life for him is, as he says, 'a new experience' – a triumph of love over greed that contrasts with his own wife's apparent indifference to his plight.

Yet it is money that is Papillon's undoing in his heroic efforts to escape. This is not just a question of plot, though he is turned in for money on both occasions.

The first escape is via the butterfly dealer who uses the convicts as collectors; he sends the butterflies to the USA, where they are made into the dye for printing dollars. This escape – immediately halted through the dealer's treachery – is thus linked to American capitalism and its dependence on slave labour. Papillon's difference from this system is emphasized by his making contact with the dealer through baring his chest, with the butterfly tattoo on it, to the dealer. He is as innocent as a butterfly – and as helpless. In the second escape, Papillon twice encounters generosity with money which helps him escape. At the leper colony, this generosity is elicited by his readiness to trust the outcast people, and, specifically, to smoke the leader's cigar. When they make a collection for him, they say they have no need of money. In the seaside, Papillon again establishes his 'human' credentials, by tattooing on the chief's chest a butterfly like his own. When the villagers disappear – as magically, as the film presents it, as they have appeared – they leave him a small bag of pearls. In both cases, the relationships (in this, the most mythic part of the film) are founded upon qualities of generosity, trust and innocence. Moreover, these are two groups of people living outside of mainstream society. The lepers are an outcast society; the Indians differentiate themselves from white society by their slaughter of the trader who tries to trick them in his dealings. As soon as Papillon re-enters 'civilized' society, as represented by the nuns, he is betrayed – the nuns take his pearls and turn him over to the authorities. Though the film is hardly a critique of capitalist or colonialist society, it does register a sense of their oppressiveness against which it can only set a more or less avowedly mythologized white male hero, and love. But Papillon leaves Dega to fulfil the modest heroic destiny the film allows him, and the film ends with the ruins of Devil's Island. Melancholy stuff indeed for a buddy blockbuster.

Movie 27/8 (1980/1)

Chapter 11

Straight acting

Heterosexuality is a public position which seems to be experienced as a purely private matter. A man I know occasionally chides me for thinking (which I don't) that people are either straight or lesbian/gay. Human sexuality, he points out, is much more complex than that; we are all (with a meaningful glance) different mixtures of hetero and homo. When this man's marriage broke up, he ricocheted within months into another, while still retaining his complex admixture of public-toilet fumblings.

Vita Sackville-West and Harold Nicolson are the most famous example of a married couple whose sexuality expressed itself in lesbian and gay bits on the side. No doubt this was as well known to cognoscenti then as it has become to devotees of high gossip now, but to the world at large their successful marriage was an affirmation of heterosexuality.

I once had a relationship with a married man. We lived in different towns and moved in rather different worlds, but in neither case were we so far apart that we did not have acquaintances in common. When it came to an end, he said the reason was that he'd discovered that people he knew, knew about us and he couldn't stand the thought of being known to be homosexual.

It's when there is a gay/lesbian aspect, as in examples like these, that it becomes evident that heterosexuality has a public dimension, it is not just a private affair. Yet the man in the first case undoubtedly experiences his sexuality as purely a matter of rich personal diversity, while Sackville-West and Nicolson, like other such couples (by no means rare), I suppose tried to be decent in their dealings with their lovers and felt that, after all, 'everyone' knew. The fact that their public acts in fact affirm heterosexuality in its most rigid form seems to escape them. At least my married lover had the grace, the wretch, to see and articulate what the loss of his heterosexual position – the fact that everyone treated him as heterosexual – would mean in terms of status, security and respect.

Heterosexuality as a social reality seems to be invisible to those who benefit from it. In part, this is because of the remorseless construction of heterosexuality as natural. If things are natural, they cannot really be questioned or scrutinized and so they fade from view. Such naturalization often characterizes how we see, and don't see, the powerful; how they see, and don't see, themselves.

We are often told that we live now in an age of diversity, that there is no longer any privileged subject of history/politics. You could have fooled me. It is true that swathes of the left feel that white, working-class men are no longer the undisputed heroes of our forward march, but, within and without that narrow culture, being heterosexual is still an undisturbed identity. Although the left now gamely includes lesbian/gay issues in its marketplace, the centrality of heterosexuality as a reference point and assumption remains secure. It is not that one is asking anyone to stop being heterosexual (well, I'm not asking that at any rate) or saying that heterosexuality is wicked. But we do need to try to see it, not just move within it as the air we breathe.

We need, in other words, to make heterosexuality strange. A student once told me that they all knew I was gay because I kept using the word 'heterosexual'. Just try dropping the term regularly into sentences and see how relentlessly the assumption of heterosexuality is built into our thought processes. Then we might be able to start considering how heterosexuality, like homosexuality, has been socially constructed.

Let me make a start on this by proposing two models, and a forgotten alternative one, of heterosexuality. I'll call these the Jane Austen, Barbara Cartland and New Woman models of heterosexuality.

The Austen model proposes heterosexuality as the coming together of opposite but complementary qualities within a context of moral equality. Thus he may have too much pride, she may have too much prejudice, but both can learn from the other, acquire respect for the dignity of pride and the energy of prejudice, modify and merge in a perfect marriage at the end of the book.

While Austen may not question the relative economic status of women and men, they are clearly seen to be humans of equal worth. In her novels, though not in my 'Austen model', personal and moral qualities may be found equally among women or men (women can be proud, men prejudiced), but generally in this construction of heterosexuality, masculinity and femininity themselves are held to be inherent opposites, requiring one another to create a perfect whole, the heterosexual couple.

The Cartland model also believes in the inherent differentness of female and male, but here the context positively luxuriates in power difference. The excitement of heterosexuality here is precisely the coming together within a relationship of such thrilling power differentials; it is him having exultant mastery over her, her blissful yielding to him, her thrilling manipulation of him from below, his charmed giving way to her attentions, that make heterosexuality tick.

The New Woman model (I can think of no hapless author to pin this to) is much less common. It proposes that it is what a man and a woman have in common that can unite them in heterosexual happiness. It is the delight in finding someone as intelligent, committed or energetic as oneself, or sharing the same sense of humour or a love of walking or an interest in science. Here anatomical and temperamental sex/gender differences are negligible, though no doubt nice; what matters is to meet one's match.

As Ruth Brandon has recently pointed out, in *New Women and Old Men*, the late-nineteenth, early-twentieth-century women who tried this out didn't get very far with the male raw material available. An ideal of union through sameness is often derided ('How boring it would be!') even though research shows that on the whole heterosexuals marry people of the same social status as themselves who look rather like them. What the New Woman model sacrifices is not only difference but power. It doesn't at the moment have much of a hope.

The baffling question is the one that Freud unaccountably never thought to ask: what do heterosexuals want? I used to assume that it must be the Austen model. It obviously wasn't the New Woman one but, I thought, surely nobody could really want the Cartland model. Within a situation of real freedom and equality (as real as we can expect to make it), I can see that lovers may play all sorts of games, turn and turn about who cuddles and is cuddled, who bites and is bitten. But the Cartland model does not even seem to want that basic context of freedom and equality, it wants the full weight of coercion and inequality in heterosocial relations reproduced in heterosexual ones. That's what I could not believe heterosexuals wanted. Now, however, I wonder.

I recently looked at some dances for heterosexual couples in musicals, clear embodiments of what the heterosexual characters in the films want and surely some indication of the state of desire in those by whom these dances are so beloved. As long as the dance suggests courtship, dating, getting to know one another, then the New Woman and Austen models prevail in the way the dancers relate to each other with their bodies. But once the dance starts to connote passion and sexuality, once the dark secret world of fucking is on the agenda, then Cartlandesque difference and domination are uppermost (and this is above all true of more recent and explicitly sexual dance films like *Dirty Dancing* and *Lambada*). All the pizzazz of identity and equality, all the exhilarating grace of complementarity that the women have in the courtship dances is diminished or lost entirely in the dances of consummation. It seems that when it comes to sex, heterosexuality cannot countenance sameness and equality.

Ethel Spector Person has argued that sexuality is a far more crucial mainstay of male identity than of female. Part of me is uneasy about her argument – does it just reproduce the idea that women are above sex? – yet there is something about it that rings true. Men may make all sorts of concessions to women's demands for sharing and equality, but there seems to be something uniquely threatening about making concessions about how you have sex. It's as if the heterosexual man's body, and indeed his penis, are his last-ditch defence against merging with the feminine, ceasing to be a male altogether. If he can't assert himself there, he's lost. And if women want men, then that's the price they'll have to pay. So the Cartland model rules.

As always with images and representations, reality is more complex and fluctuating. The actual practice of heterosexuality must to some extent outstrip the cultural models available to it. Yet it would be absurd to assume that those models are of no account whatsoever. It will only be by learning to see them that we will be able to rethink and refeel sexuality, that we will be able to change the sexual order itself. As long as we don't, heterosexuals will continue to be locked into expectations of joy through power and lesbians and gay men will continue to be bits on the side of society.

Marxism Today (August 1990)

REFERENCES

Brandon, Ruth (1990) *The New Women and the Old Men*, London: Secker & Warburg.
Person, Ethel Spector (1980) 'Sexuality as the Mainstay of Identity: Psychoanalytic Perspectives', *Signs* 5 (4): 605–30.

FURTHER READING

Dyer, Richard (1993) '"I Seem to Find the Happiness I Seek": Heterosexuality and Dance in the Musical', in Thomas, Helen (ed.) *Dance, Gender and Culture*, London: Macmillan.

Chapter 12

A Passage to India

A Passage to India (1985) is a liberal film. There was a time on the left when to call something liberal was to condemn it out of hand as weak, equivocating, untheorized, unmaterialist and, of course, bourgeois. Liberalism is indeed all of those things, but in the age of Thatcher and Reagan we may need to be a little less quick off the mark about it – right now we need all the liberals we can get.

The problem is that there's liberalism and liberalism, or, I'm tempted to say, there's E. M. Forster's liberalism and there's David Lean's. I don't as a rule much care for looking at a film in terms of the book it is based upon. A film is a film, good or bad in its own terms and not for the degree to which it matches its literary source – and it is even more important to stick to this principle when the book is, like *A Passage to India* (1924), a 'classic', nay, a 'set text' all the way up the exam system. But there are one or two points where a film–book comparison here does indicate the difference between a valuable and honourable liberalism and a smug, stifling one.

The key incident in the novel is the visit of Aziz, a local doctor, and Adela, a young English woman recently arrived in India, to the Marabar caves. Something happens in the caves, and shortly afterwards Aziz is taken to court on an assault charge. In the book you never know for certain what happened in the caves – Aziz may have made a pass at Adela, or raped her, or she may have imagined that he did, or something else quite other may have happened. Not only is what happened not described, you don't get to know later what really took place. The film too does not show what happened in the caves, but you are never really left in any doubt that Aziz did not so much as lay a finger on Adela. The charm of Victor Bannerjee's playing of Aziz and the fact that the two good-and-truthful characters, Mrs Moore (Peggy Ashcroft) and Fielding (James Fox), believe in him so steadfastly while all manner of blimpish buffoons condemn him, combine to rob what happened in the caves of its disturbing ambiguity. Even if you never find out what did happen in the caves, at least you don't need to worry that it might have been something sexual.

This shift of emphasis is one characteristic of much white liberalism. We have a problem in dealing with black sexuality – we have learnt well that it is a slur on black people to credit them with a dangerous, rampant, seething sexuality, as so much racist and imperialist thought does. That kind of attitude is itself neatly mocked in the courtroom scene in the film. So anxious are we not to be associated with this attitude however that we then fall back on whitewashed images of black sexuality as almost non-existent in its innocence. In other words, in the film, this kind of liberalism cannot allow even the possibility that Aziz may have done something sexual because it must protest that he is innocent – whereas the intriguing and disturbing point about the incident in the book is that Aziz's undoubted innocence may none the less include his sexuality. He is inno-cent of the torrid and sordid sexuality the British ascribe to him, but he may indeed have made love to Adela. We cannot know, because in a sense we are so blinkered by our uptight, upright notions of sexuality that we cannot comprehend the way it is so differently constructed in other cultures.

In the book this also links in with the question of sexual feeling between men. The film plays this down – it's hard even to say whether the shots through the glazed glass of Fielding taking a shower when Aziz first visits him, and of Aziz putting on eye makeup and magnificent Indian attire when Fielding visits him at the end of the film, are meant to have an erotic charge or not. There is certainly no development of the undertow of gay feeling that you get in the book. This kind of liberalism is happier showing friendship between people of different races if it can leave out of account the confusing, disturbing note of sexuality, especially if, as here, that sexuality is ineluctably caught up in the western imagination with notions of the deviant and the perverse.

It is not only the trouble of sexuality that is at issue. The caves represent the unknowability of Indian culture. This could just be the old cliché of the inscrutable, inexpressibly exotic and mysterious character of the Orient, and perhaps both book and film do have something of this in them. Perhaps, indeed, it is impossible for western people to speak, write or film eastern cultures without getting tied up in this particular rhetoric of 'Orientalism'. In the novel, however, there is also a strong sense of the impertinence of the imperial assumption that one can have any easy access to the thought and feeling patterns of another culture. The film has found no way to convey this, so that the caves come to seem simply meaningless – whereas the point is that they do have meaning but not one that the British can fathom.

The recognition of an irreducible barrier of difference between cultures also has a political dimension that gets lost in the film. This is most clearly indicated by the treatment of the final meeting in both book and film between Aziz and Fielding. In the book, when the two part there is an image of their two horses swerving apart even as they ride towards each other. The context makes it clear that this symbolizes the ineradicable, essentially political gulf that separates the two men, despite their feeling for each other. This is replaced in the film with a touching reunion between the two men and a tearful parting (though neither of them cries, of course) suggesting that, none the less, everything is all right now. The book's image of the swerving horses would have made a beautiful film image, and of the kind that David Lean has often used brilliantly in his films. It has been objected that the book was written before Indian independence and that now friendship may be affirmed between the two 'free' nations. Yet not only is the film still set before independence and thus still under the direct impact of imperialism, but we also still live scarred by that imperialism, as the situation of Indian people in Britain today testifies.

David Lean's film might indeed have affirmed such a friendship against the odds of the politics that would divide it. Many of his best, most searingly moving films – *Brief Encounter, Summer Madness, Ryan's Daughter* – are just such evocations of love achieved against the barriers that society has put up against it. What is also characteristic of these films is that society wins in the end – love is a brief glorious moment snatched in the teeth of division and oppression. Yet in *A Passage to India*, perhaps in part because Lean did not care to speak the name of the love between Fielding and Aziz, we end with a smug reconciliation between the two men, an easy decent-chaps-together bit and never mind the imperialism. Part of the film's smugness is also in its style. It is of course an extraordinarily accomplished, crafted film. The photography is beautiful (in the very best colour supplement way), ravishingly lovely, with the kind of luminousness that you only get with perfect colour prints on a big screen. The timing of each shot is impeccable, lingering long enough to register the beauty of a landscape but not so long as to hold up the unfolding of the story. The acting is nuanced, detailed, carefully observed, exquisitely rounded. Everything in the film is in place – which also means that everything in the film is neatly parcelled up.

It is instructive to compare it not with the novel but with the television version of *The Jewel in the Crown* (1982). This too had lovely photography, superb acting and so on, but what it also had was a kind of awkwardness. Scenes would come to an abrupt end or go on longer than seemed necessary for the story; episodes would end on a disconcertingly sudden freeze frame; there were quite long stretches of dialogue that, when they were over, you realized had been quite opaque as far as understanding quite what had been going on between characters, a feeling intensified by the performances, full of pauses and shifting and sudden loudness and looking away. That sense of a neatly rounded off, unproblematic world of domination and imperialism that comes across in the film of *A Passage to India* was not so with *Jewel in the Crown*, where the sense of the sheer difficulty of the exercise of liberalism and understanding remained uppermost.

One of liberalism's cardinal virtues is tolerance, and it is not one that much of the left has a good track record on. There is a difference however between tolerance based on a complacent assumption that we're all the same anyway and tolerance that acknowledges the stubborn core of differences between peoples. The first form of tolerance imposes the liberal's own sense of how people are in her/his own world on to other parts of the world (including other classes, minorities, even the opposite sex) – it is this self-satisfied liberal tolerance that assumes western Marxism is entirely appropriate to the situations of the Third World, or that women or blacks or gays in political parties do not inhabit specific and different situations requiring at least some of the time separate organization. The other kind of tolerance acknowledges that one cannot just enter and understand difference, and withdraws from judgement or the interference of 'understanding'. The film *A Passage to India* invites us to take up the former tolerance, and this matters. It is not a wrangle over protecting a 'great author's' vision, it is not worrying about a story set in the dim and distant past. In multi-cultural contemporary Britain, in a world still entangled in imperialisms of many kinds, we need more than ever to foster the real tolerance of real difference.

Marxism Today (April 1985)

FURTHER READING

Rushdie, Salman (1992) 'Outside the Whale', in *Imaginary Homeland*, London: Penguin/Granta Books, 125–38.

Chapter 13

White

This is an article about a subject that, much of the time as I've been writing it, seems not to be there as a subject at all. Trying to think about the representation of whiteness as an ethnic category in mainstream film is difficult, partly because white power secures its dominance by seeming not to be anything in particular but also because, when whiteness *qua* whiteness does come into focus, it is often revealed as emptiness, absence, denial or even a kind of death.

It is, all the same, important to try to make some headway with grasping whiteness as a culturally constructed category. 'Images of' studies have looked at groups defined as oppressed, marginal or subordinate – women, the working class, ethnic and other minorities (e.g., lesbians and gay men, disabled people, the elderly). The impulse for such work lies in the sense that how such groups are represented is part of the process of their oppression, marginalization or subordination. The range and fertility of such work has put those groups themselves centre-stage in both analytical and campaigning activity, and highlighted the issue of representation as politics. It has, however, had one serious drawback, long recognized in debates about women's studies. Looking, with such passion and single-mindedness, at non-dominant groups has had the effect of reproducing the sense of the oddness, differentness, exceptionality of these groups, the feeling that they are departures from the norm. Meanwhile the norm has carried on as if it is the natural, inevitable, ordinary way of being human.

Some efforts are now being made to rectify this, to see that the norm too is constructed, although only with masculinity has anything approaching a proliferation of texts begun. Perhaps it is worth signalling here, before proceeding, two of the pitfalls in the path of such work, two convolutions that especially characterize male writing about masculinity – guilt and me-too-ism. Let me state that, while writing here as a white person about whiteness, I do not mean either to display the expiation of my guilt about being white nor to hint that it is also awful to be white (because it is an inadequate, limiting definition of being human, because feeling guilty is such a burden). Studies of dominance by the dominant should not deny the place of the writer in relation to what s/he is writing about it, but nor should they be the green light for self-recrimination or trying to get in on the act.

Power in contemporary society habitually passes itself off as embodied in the normal as opposed to the superior (cf. Marcuse 1964). This is common to all forms of power, but it works in a peculiarly seductive way with whiteness, because of the way it seems rooted, in commonsense thought, in things other than ethnic difference. The very terms we use to describe the major ethnic divide presented by western society, 'black' and 'white', are imported from and naturalized by other discourses. Thus it is said (even in liberal textbooks) that there are inevitable associations of white with light and therefore safety, and black with dark and therefore danger, and that this explains racism (whereas one might well argue about the safety of the cover of darkness and the danger of exposure to the light); again, and with more justice, people point to the Judaeo-Christian use of white and black to symbolize good and evil, as carried still in such expressions as 'a black mark', 'white magic', 'to blacken the character' and so on (cf. Jordan 1969 and Fryer 1984). I'd like to look at another aspect of commonsensical conflations of black and white as natural and ethnic categories by considering ideas of what colour is.

I was taught the scientific difference between black and white at primary school. It seemed a fascinating paradox. Black, which, because you had to add it to paper to make a picture, I had always thought of as a colour, was, it turned out, nothingness, the absence of all colour; whereas white, which looked just like empty space (or blank paper), was, apparently, all the colours there were put together. No doubt such explanations of colour have long been outmoded; what interests me is how they manage to touch on the construction of the ethnic categories of black and white in dominant representation. In the realm of categories, black is always marked as a colour (as the term 'coloured' egregiously acknowledges), and is always particularizing; whereas white is not anything really, not an identity, not a particularizing quality, because it is everything – white is no colour because it is all colours.

This property of whiteness, to be everything and nothing, is the source of its representational power. On the one hand, as one of the people in the video *Being White*[1] observes, white domination is reproduced by the way that white people 'colonise the definition of normal'. Paul Gilroy similarly spells out the political consequences, in the British context, of the way that whiteness both disappears behind and is subsumed into other identities. He discusses the way that the language of 'the nation' aims to be unifying, permitting even socialists an appeal in terms of 'we' and 'our' 'beyond the margins of sectional interest', but goes on to observe that:

there is a problem in these plural forms: who do they include, or, more precisely for our purposes, do they help to reproduce blackness and Englishness as mutually exclusive categories? . . . why are contemporary appeals to 'the people' in danger of transmitting themselves as appeals to the white people?

(1987: 55–6)[2]

On the other hand, if the invisibility of whiteness colonizes the definition of other norms – class, gender, heterosexuality, nationality and so on – it also masks whiteness as itself a category. White domination is then hard to grasp in terms of the characteristics and practices of white people. No one would deny that, at the very least, there are advantages to being white in western societies, but it is only avowed racists who have a theory which attributes this to inherent qualities of white people. Otherwise, whiteness is presented more as a case of historical accident, rather than a characteristic cultural/historical construction, achieved through white domination.

The colourless multi-colouredness of whiteness secures white power by making it hard, especially for white people and their media, to 'see' whiteness. This, of course, also makes it hard to analyse. It is the way that black people are marked as black (are not just 'people') in representation that has made it relatively easy to analyse their representation, whereas white people – not there as a category and everywhere everything as a fact – are difficult, if not impossible, to analyse *qua* white. The subject seems to fall apart in your hands as soon as you begin. Any instance of white representation is always immediately something more specific – *Brief Encounter* is not about white people, it is about English middle-class people; *The Godfather* is not about white people, it is about Italian-American people; but *The Color Purple* is about black people, before it is about poor, southern US people.

This problem clearly faced the makers of *Being White*, a pioneering attempt to confront the notion of white identity. The opening vox pop sequence vividly illustrates the problem. Asked how they would define themselves, the white interviewees refer easily to gender, age, nationality or looks but never to ethnicity. Asked if they think of themselves as white, most say that they don't, though one or two speak of being 'proud' or 'comfortable' to be white. In an attempt to get some white people to explore what being white means, the video assembles a group to talk about it and it is here that the problem of white people's inability to see whiteness appears intractable. Sub-categories of whiteness (Irishness, Jewishness, Britishness) take over, so that the particularity of whiteness itself begins to disappear; then gradually, it seems almost inexorably, the participants settle in to talking with confidence about what they know: stereotypes of black people.

Yet perhaps this slide towards talking about blackness gives us a clue as to where we might begin to see whiteness – where its difference from blackness is inescapable and at issue. I shall look here at examples of mainstream cinema whose narratives are marked by the fact of ethnic difference. Other approaches likely to yield interesting results include: the study of the characterization of whites in Third World or diaspora cinema; images of the white race in avowedly racist and fascist cinema; the use of the 'commutation test' (Thompson 1978), the imaginary substitution of black for white performers in films such as *Brief Encounter*, say, or *Ordinary People* (if these are unimaginable played by black actors, what does this tell us about the characteristics of whiteness?) or, related to this, consideration of what ideas of whiteness are implied by such widespread observations as that Sidney Poitier or Diana Ross, say, are to all intents and purposes 'white'. What all these approaches share, however, is reference to that which is not white, as if only non-whiteness can give whiteness any substance. The reverse is not the case – studies of images of blacks, Native Americans, Jews and other ethnic minorities do not need the comparative element that seems at this stage indispensable for the study of whites.

The representation of white *qua* white begins to come into focus – in mainstream cinema, for a white spectator – in films in which non-white characters play a significant role. I want to look at three very different examples here – *Jezebel* (USA, Warner Brothers, 1938), *Simba* (GB, Rank Studios, 1955) and *Night of the Living Dead* (USA, 1969). Each is characteristic of the particular genre and period to which it belongs. *Jezebel* is a large-budget Hollywood feature film (said to have been intended to rival *Gone with the Wind*) built around a female star, Bette Davis; its spectacular pleasures are those of costume and decor, of gracious living, and its emotional pleasures those of tears. *Simba* is a film made as part of Rank's bid to produce films that might successfully challenge Hollywood at the box office, built around a male star, Dirk Bogarde; its spectacular pleasures are those of the travelogue, its emotional ones excitement and also the gratification of seeing 'issues' (here, the Mau-Mau in Kenya) being dealt with. *Night of the Living Dead* is a cheap, independently-produced horror film with no stars; its spectacular and emotional pleasures are those of shock, disgust and suspense, along with the evident political or social symbolism that has aided its cult reputation.

The differences between the three films are important and will inform the ways in which they represent whiteness. Yet there is some point in trying to see continuity across three, none the less significantly different, films. There is no doubt that part of the strength and resilience of stereotypes of non-dominant groups resides in their variation and flexibility – stereotypes are seldom found in a pure form and this is part of the process by which they are naturalized, kept alive (Perkins 1979; Neale 1979/80).

Yet the strength of white representation, as I've suggested, is the apparent absence altogether of the typical, the sense that being white is co-terminous with the endless plenitude of human diversity. If we are to see the historical, cultural and political limitations (to put it mildly) of white world domination, it is important to see similarities, typicalities, within the seemingly infinite variety of white representation.

All three films share a perspective that associates whiteness with order, rationality, rigidity, qualities brought out by the contrast with black disorder, irrationality and looseness. It is their take on this which differs. *Simba* operates with a clear black–white binarism, holding out the possibility that black people can learn white values but fearing that white people will be engulfed by blackness. *Jezebel* is far more ambivalent, associating blackness with the defiance of its female protagonist, whom it does not know whether to condemn or adore. *Night* takes the hint of critique of whiteness in *Jezebel* and takes it to its logical conclusion, where whiteness represents not only rigidity but death.

What these films also share, which helps to sharpen further the sense of whiteness in them, is a situation in which white domination is contested, openly in the text of *Simba*, and explicitly acknowledged in *Jezebel*. The narrative of *Simba* is set in motion by the Mau-Mau challenge to British occupation, which also occasions set pieces of debate on the issues of white rule and black responses to it; the imminent decline of slavery is only once or twice referred to directly in *Jezebel*, but the film can assume the audience knows that slavery was soon ostensibly to disappear from the southern states. Both films are suffused with the sense of white rule being at an end, a source of definite sorrow in *Simba* but in *Jezebel* producing that mixture of disapproval and nostalgia characteristic of the white representation of the ante-bellum South. *Night* makes no direct reference to the state of ethnic play but, as I shall argue below, it does make implicit reference to the black uprisings that were part of the historical context of its making, and which many believed would alter irrevocably the nature of power relations between black and white people in the USA.

The presence of black people in all three films allows one to see whiteness as whiteness, and in this way relates to the existential psychology that is at the origins of the interest in 'otherness' as an explanatory concept in the representation of ethnicity (Fanon 1986; Saïd 1978; Bhatha 1983). Existential psychology, principally in the work of Jean-Paul Sartre, had proposed a model of human growth whereby the individual self becomes aware of itself as a self by perceiving its difference from others. It was other writers who suggested that this process, supposedly at once individual and universal, was in fact socially specific – Simone de Beauvoir arguing that it has to do with the construction of the male ego, Frantz Fanon relating it to the colonial encounter of white and black. What I want to stress here is less this somewhat metaphysical dimension (cf. Parry 1987), more the material basis for the shifts and anxieties in the representation of whiteness suggested by *Simba, Jezebel* and *Night*.

The three films relate to situations in which whites hold power in society, but are materially dependent upon black people. All three films suggest an awareness of this dependency – weakly in *Simba*, strongly but still implicitly in *Jezebel*, inescapably in *Night*. It is this actual dependency of white on black in a context of continued white power and privilege that throws the legitimacy of white domination into question. What is called for is a demonstration of the virtues of whiteness that would justify continued domination, but this is a problem if whiteness is also invisible, everything and nothing. It is from this that the films' fascinations derive. I shall discuss them here in the order in which they most clearly attempt to hang on to some justification of whiteness, starting, then, with *Simba* and ending with *Night*.

SIMBA

Simba is a characteristic product of the British cinema between about 1945 and 1965 – an entertainment film 'dealing with' a serious issue (Hill 1986). It is a colonial adventure film, offering the standard narrative pleasures of adventure with a tale of personal growth. The hero, Alan (Bogarde), arrives in Kenya from England to visit his brother on his farm, finds he has been killed by the Mau-Mau and stays to sort things out (keep the farm going, find out who killed his brother, quell the Mau-Mau). Because the Mau-Mau were a real administrative and ideological problem for British imperialism at the time of the film's making, *Simba* also has to construct a serious discursive context for these pleasures (essentially a moral one, to do with the proper way to treat native peoples, toughness versus niceness). It does this partly through debates and discussions, partly through characters clearly representing what the film takes to be the range of possible angles on the subject (the bigoted whites, the liberal whites, the British-educated black man, the despotic black chief) but above all through the figure of the hero, whose adventures and personal growth are occasioned, even made possible, through the process of engaging with the late colonial situation. The way this situation is structured by the film and the way Alan/Bogarde rises to the occasion display the qualities of whiteness.

Simba is founded on the 'Manicheism delirium' identified by Fanon as characteristic of the colonialist sensibility (1986: 1); it takes what Paul Gilroy refers to as an 'absolutist view of black and white cultures, as fixed, mutually impermeable expressions of racial and national identity, [which] is a ubiquitous theme in racial "common sense" ' (1987: 6). The film is organized around a rigid binarism, with white standing for modernity, reason, order, stability, and black standing for backwardness, irrationality, chaos and violence. This binarism is reproduced in every detail of the film's

Figure 13.1 Orderly rows, full light, debate – the white meeting in *Simba*

mise-en-scène. A sequence of two succeeding scenes illustrates this clearly – a meeting of the white settlers to discuss the emergency, followed by a meeting of the Mau-Mau. The whites' meeting (figure 13.1) takes place in early evening, in a fully lit room; characters who speak are shot with standard high-key lighting so that they are fully visible; everyone sits in rows and although there is disagreement, some of it hot-tempered and emotional, it is expressed in grammatical discourse in a language the British viewer can understand; moreover, the meeting consists of nothing but speech. The black meeting, on the other hand, takes place at dead of night, out of doors, with all characters in shadow; even the Mau-Mau leader is lit with extreme sub-expressionist lighting that dramatizes and distorts his face; grouping is in the form of a broken, uneven circle; what speech there is is ritualized, not reasoned, and remains untranslated (and probably in no authentic language anyway), and most vocal sounds are whooping, gabbling and shrieking; the heart of the meeting is in any case not speech, but daubing with blood and entrails and scarring the body. The return to whiteness after this sequence is once again a return to daylight, a dissolve to the straight lines of European fencing and vegetable plots.

The emphasis on the visible and bounded in this mise-en-scène (maintained throughout the film) has to do with the importance of fixity in the stereotyping of others – clear boundaries are characteristic of things white (lines, grids, not speaking till someone else has finished and so on), and also what keeps whites clearly distinct from blacks. The importance of the process of boundary establishment and maintenance has long been recognized in discussions of stereotyping and representation (Bhabha 1983; Dyer 1993; Gilman 1985). This process is functional for dominant groups, but through it the capacity to set boundaries becomes a characteristic attribute of such groups, endlessly reproduced in ritual, costume, language and, in cinema, mise-en-scène. Thus, whites and men (especially) become characterized by 'boundariness' (cf. Chodorow 1978).

Simba's binarism is in the broadest sense racist, but not in the narrower sense of operating with a notion of intrinsic and unalterable biological bases for differences between peoples (Banton 1977).[3] It is informed rather by a kind of evolutionism, the idea of a path of progress already followed by whites but in principle open to all human beings – hence the elements in the binarism of modernity versus backwardness. Such evolutionism raises the possibility of blacks becoming like whites, and it is the belief in this possibility that underpins the views of the liberal characters in the film, Mary (Virginia McKenna) and Dr Hughes (Joseph Tomelty), the latter pleading with his fellow settlers at the meeting to 'reason', not with the Mau-Mau but with the other Africans, who are not beyond the reach of rational discussion. The possibility is further embodied in the character of Peter Karanja (Earl Cameron), the son of the local chief (Orlando Martins), who has trained to be a doctor and is now running a surgery in the village. The film is at great pains to establish that Peter is indeed reasonable, rational, humane, liberal. It is always made quite clear to the viewer that this is so and the representatives of liberalism always believe in him; it is the other whites who do not trust him, and one of Alan's moral lessons is to learn to respect Peter's worth. It seems then that part of the film is ready to take the liberal evolutionist position. Yet it is also significant that the spokespeople for liberalism (niceness and reason) are socially subordinate: a woman and a Welsh doctor (played for comic eccentricity most of the time); and that liberalism fails, with its representatives (Mary, Peter and now won-over Alan) left at the end of the film crouched in the flames of Alan's farm, rescued from the Mau-Mau in the nick of time by the arrival of the white militia, and Peter dying from wounds inflicted on him by the Mau-Mau (represented as a black mob (figure 13.2)). Although with its head, as it were, the film endorses the possibility of a black person becoming 'white', this is in fact deeply disturbing, setting in motion the anxiety attendant on any loosening of the fixed visibility of the colonized other. This anxiety is established from the start of the film and is the foundation of its narrative.

Figure 13.2 Loose formation, darkness, yelling – the black uprising in *Simba*

As is customary in colonial adventure films, *Simba* opens with a panoramic shot of the land, accompanied here by birdsong and the sound of an African man singing. While not especially lush or breathtaking, it is peaceful and attractive. A cry of pain interrupts this mood and we see the man who has been singing stop, get off his bicycle and walk towards its source to find a white man lying covered in blood on the ground. The black man kneels by his side, apparently about to help him, but then, to the sound of a drum-roll on the soundtrack, draws his machete and plunges it (off screen) into the wounded man. He then walks back to his bike and rides off. Here is encapsulated the fear that ensues if you can't see black men behaving as black men should, the deceptiveness of a black man in western clothes riding a bike. This theme is then reiterated throughout the film. Which of the servants can be trusted? How can you tell who is Mau-Mau and who not? Why should Alan trust Peter?

This opening sequence is presented in one long take, using panning. As the man rides off, the sound of a plane is heard, the camera pans up and there is the first cut of the film, to a plane flying through the clouds. There follows (with credits over) a series of aerial shots of the African landscape, in one of which a plane's shadow is seen, and ending with shots of white settlement and then the plane coming to land. Here is another aspect of the film's binarism. The credit sequence uses the dynamics of editing following the more settled feel of the pre-credit long take; it uses aerial shots moving through space, rather than pans with their fixed vantage point; it emphasizes the view from above, not that from the ground, and the modernity of air travel after the primitivism of the machete. It also brings the hero to Africa (as we realize when we see Bogarde step off in the first post-credit shot), brings the solution to the problems of deceptive, unfixed appearances set up by the pre-credit sequence.

Simba's binarism both establishes the differences between black and white and creates the conditions for the film's narrative pleasures – the disturbance of the equilibrium of clear-cut binarism, the resultant conflict that the hero has to resolve. His ability to resolve it is part of his whiteness, just as whiteness is identified in the dynamism of the credit sequence (which in turn relates to the generic expectations of adventure) and in the narrative of personal growth that any colonial text with pretensions also has. The empire provided a narrative space for the realization of manhood, as both action and maturation (Hall 1981). The colonial landscape is expansive, enabling the hero to roam and giving us the entertainment of action; it is unexplored, giving him the task of discovery and us the pleasures of mystery; it is uncivilized, needing taming, providing the spectacle of power; it is difficult and dangerous, testing his machismo, providing us with suspense. In other words, the colonial landscape provides the occasion for the realization of white male virtues, which are not qualities of being but of doing – acting, discovering, taming, conquering. At the same time, colonialism, as a social, political and economic system, even in fictions, also carries with it challenges of responsibility, of the establishment and maintenance of order, of the application of reason and authority to situations. These, too, are qualities of white manhood that are realized in the process of the colonial text, and very explicitly in *Simba*. When Alan arrives at Nairobi, he is met by Mary, a woman to whom he had proposed when she was visiting England; she had turned him down, telling him, as he recalls on the drive to his brother's farm, that he had 'no sense of responsibility'. Now he realizes that she was right; in the course of the film he will learn to be responsible in the process of dealing with the Mau-Mau, and this display of growth will win him Mary.

But this is a late colonial text, characterized by a recognition that the empire is at an end, and not unaware of some kinds of liberal critique of colonialism. So *Simba* takes a turn that is far more fully explored by, say, *Black Narcissus* (1947) or the Granada television adaptation of *The Jewel in the Crown* (1982). Here, maturity involves the melancholy recognition of failure. This is explicitly stated, by Sister Clodagh in *Black Narcissus*, to be built into the geographical conditions in which the nuns seek to establish their civilizing mission ('I couldn't stop the wind from blowing'); it is endlessly repeated by the nice whites in *The Jewel in the Crown* ('There's nothing I can do!') and symbolized in the lace shawl with butterflies 'caught in the net' that keeps being brought out by the characters. I have already suggested the ways in which liberalism is marginalized and shown to fail in *Simba*. More than this, the hero also fails to realize the generically pro-mised adventure experiences: he is unable to keep his late brother's farm going, nor does he succeed in fighting off a man stealing guns from his house; he fails to catch the fleeing leader of the Mau-Mau, and is unable to prevent them from destroying his house and shooting Peter. The film ends with his property in flames and – a touch common to British social conscience films – with a shot of a young black boy who symbolizes the only possible hope for the future.

The repeated failure of narrative achievement goes along with a sense of white helplessness in the face of the Mau-Mau (the true black threat), most notably in the transition between the two meeting scenes discussed above. Alan has left the meeting in anger because one of the settlers has criticized the way his brother had dealt with the Africans (too soft); Mary joins him, to comfort him. At the end of their conversation, there is a two-shot of them, with Mary saying of the situation, 'it's like a flood, we're caught in it'. This is accompanied by the sound of drums and is immediately followed by a slow dissolve to black people walking through the night towards the Mau-Mau meeting. The drums and the dissolve enact Mary's words, the whites 'caught' in the encroachment of blackness.

Simba is, then, an endorsement of the moral superiority of white values of reason, order and boundedness, yet suggests a loss of belief in their efficacy. This is a familiar trope of conservatism. At moments, though, there are glimpses of something else, achieved inadvertently perhaps through the casting of Dirk Bogarde. It becomes explicit in the scene between Mary and Alan just mentioned, when Alan says to Mary, 'I was suddenly afraid of what I was feeling', referring to the anger and hatred that the whole situation is bringing out in him and, as Mary says, everyone else. The implication is that the situation evokes in whites the kind of irrational violence supposedly specific to blacks. Of course, being white means being able to repress it and this is what we seem to see in Alan throughout the film. Such repression constitutes the stoic glory of the imperial hero, but there is something about Bogarde in the part that makes it seem less than admirable or desirable. Whether this is suggested by his acting style, still and controlled, yet with fiercely grinding jaws, rigidly clenched hands and very occasional sudden outbursts of shouting, or by the way Rank was grooming him against the grain of his earlier, sexier image (including its gay overtones) (Medhurst 1986), it suggests a notion of whiteness as repression that leads us neatly on to *Jezebel*.

JEZEBEL

Like *Simba*, *Jezebel* depicts a white society characterized by order and rigidity, here expressed principally through codes of behaviour and rules of conduct embodied in set piece receptions, dinner parties and balls. This does contrast with the bare glimpses we get of black life in the film, but *Jezebel* also explores the ways in which whiteness is related to blackness, materially and emotionally dependent on it yet still holding sway over it.

Compositionally, *Jezebel* frequently foregrounds black people – scenes often open with the camera moving from a black person (a woman selling flowers in New Orleans (figure 13.3), a servant carrying juleps, a boy pulling on a rope to operate a ceiling fan) across or towards white characters; black people often intrude into the frame while white characters talk. This is particularly noticeable during a dinner-table discussion of the future of slavery; when one of the characters, Pres (Henry Fonda), says that the South will be defeated by machines triumphing over 'unskilled slave labour', the chief black character, Cato (Lou Payton), leans across our field of vision to pour Pres's wine, literally embodying the fact of slave labour. The film's insistence upon the presence of black people is important in its perception and construction of the white South. As Jim Pines puts it, 'black characters do not occupy a significant dramatic function in the film, but their social role nevertheless plays an explicit and relevant part in the conflict that arises between the principal white characters' (Pines 1975: 59).

Jezebel is distantly related, through the sympathies of its stars, director and production studio, to progressive ideas on race, making it, as Pines says, 'within the plantation movie tradition . . . undoubtedly the most liberal-inclined' (ibid.: 55; cf. Cripps 1977: 299, 304). These ideas have to do with the belief or suspicion that black people have in some sense more 'life' than whites. This idea, and its ambivalences, have a very long history which cannot detain us here. It springs from ideas of the closeness of non-European (and even non-metropolitan) peoples to nature, ideas which were endemic to those processes of European expansion variously termed exploration, nation building and colonialism (Robinson 1983). Expansion into other lands placed the humans encountered there as part of the fauna of those lands, to be construed either as the forces of nature that had to be subjugated or, for liberals, the model of sweet natural Man uncontaminated by civilization. At the same time, ideas of nature have become central to western thought about being human, such that concepts of human life itself have become inextricable from concepts of nature. Thus the idea that non-whites are more natural than whites also comes to suggest that they have more 'life', a logically meaningless but commonsensically powerful notion.

Jezebel relates to a specific liberal variation on this way of thinking, a tradition in which *Uncle Tom's Cabin* and the Harlem Renaissance are key reference points (Fredrickson 1972; Lewis 1981), as is the role of Annie in

Figure 13.3 A marginal but foregrounded black figure in *Jezebel*

Sirk's *Imitation of Life*. Ethel Mannin's statement may be taken as emblematic:

> It is of course that feeling for life which is the secret of the Negro people, as surely as it is the lack of it, and slow atrophy of the capacity to live emotionally, which will be the ultimate decadence of the white civilised people.

(1930: 157)

'Life' here tends to mean the body, the emotions, sensuality and spirituality; it is usually explicitly counterposed to the mind and the intellect, with the implication that white people's over-investment in the cerebral is cutting them off from life and leading them to crush the life out of others and out of nature itself. The implicit counterposition is, of course, 'death', a point to which I shall return in the discussion of *Night of the Living Dead*.

Jezebel is generally, and rightly, understood to be about the taming of a woman who refuses to live by the Old South's restrictive codes of femininity. It is a clear instance of Molly Haskell's characterization of one of the available models for strong women's roles in classic Hollywood movies, the 'superfemale', who is 'too ambitious and intelligent for the docile role society has decreed she play' but remains 'exceedingly "feminine" and flirtatious' and 'within traditional society', turning her energies on those around her, 'with demonic results' (1974: 214). Davis's character, Julie, is strong, defiant of convention (for example, striding into the bank, a place that women do not enter), refusing to behave in the genteel way her fiancé, Pres, requires of her. The trajectory of the narrative is her punishment and moral growth, in two stages. She learns to conceal her defiance and energy beneath an assumption of femininity, but this is still not enough, since it is still there in the malignant form indicated by Haskell; it is only by literally sacrificing herself (accompanying Pres, who has caught yellow jack fever, to Red Island, where fever victims are isolated) that the film is able to reach a satisfactory, transcendentally punishing climax. All of this is entirely understandable within a gender frame of reference; but the film also relates Julie's energies to blackness, suggesting that her trajectory is a specifically white, as well as female, one.

The most famous scene in the film is the Olympus Ball, at which all the unmarried women wear white. Julie, to embarrass Pres and to cock a snook at out-dated convention ('This is 1852, not the Dark Ages – girls don't have to simper about in white just 'cos they're not married'), decides to wear a red dress (figure 13.4). The immediate scandal is not just the refusal to conform and uphold the celebration of virginity that the white dress code represents but the sexual connotations of the dress itself, satin and red, connotations made explicit in a scene at the dressmaker's ('Saucy, isn't it?', says Julie; 'And vulgar', says her aunt, with which Julie enthusiastically concurs). This is the dress of Julie's that her black maid Zette (Theresa Harris) most covets, and after the ball Julie gives it to her. It is precisely its *colourfulness* that, stereotyping informs us, draws Zette – the dress is 'marked' as coloured, a definite, bold colour heightened by a flashy fabric, just as black representation is. Thus what appears to be symbolism (white for virginity, colour for sex) within a universally applicable communication circuit becomes ethnically specific. The primary association of white with chastity is inextricably tied to not being dark and colourful, not being non-white, and the defiance and vitality narratively associated with Julie's wearing of the dress is associated with the qualities embodied by black women, qualities that Julie as a white woman must not display, or even have. Of course, the red dress looks merely dark in this black and white film.

Wearing the dress causes a rift between Julie and Pres; shortly after, he leaves for the North on business. By the time he returns, Julie has learned to behave as a white woman should. Once again, the specific whiteness of this is revealed through the figure of Zette. There is, for instance, a scene

Figure 13.4 Jezebel: the red (dark) dress at the white ball

in which Julie is getting ready for the arrival of Pres at a house party at her aunt's plantation. In her room she moves restlessly about, with Zette hanging on to her as she tries to undo Julie's dress at the back; Zette's movements are entirely determined by Julie's but Zette is attending to the basic clothing while Julie is just fussing about. When Julie thinks she hears a carriage coming, she sends Zette to check; Zette runs from the room, and the film cuts to the huge hallway, showing us all of Zette's rapid descent of the stairs and run to the door, before cutting again to show her calling out to the man and boy in livery waiting for carriages at the gate. This apparently unnecessarily elongated sequence not only helps whip up excitement and anticipation at Pres's arrival, but also gives Julie time to take off one dress and put on another, a potentially titillating sight that would not be shown in this kind of film in this period. But using a sequence centred on a black woman is not only a device to heighten suspense and bypass a taboo image – it works as seamlessly well as it does because it is also appropriate to show a black woman here.

By this stage in the film, Julie has learned the behaviour appropriate to a white woman in her position. Earlier in the film she openly expressed her passion and defiance; now, awaiting Pres, she has learned to behave as she should. She no longer expresses feeling – she 'lives' through Zette. Zette has to express excited anticipation, not in speech but in physical action, running the length of a long stair and spacious hallway. It is Zette's excited body in action that we see, instead of Julie's body disrobed and enrobed. When Julie hears the servants at the gate call out, 'Carriage is coming!', she sends Zette to the window to see if it is Pres. The excitement mounts as the carriage draws near. There is a rapid montage of black people: Zette shot from below at a dynamic angle looking for the carriage, the servants at the gate no longer still but the man moving about, the boy leaping in anticipation, and crowds of hitherto unseen black children running to the gate, jumping and cavorting. Meanwhile Julie remains perfectly still, only her eyes, in characteristic Davis fashion, darting and dilating with suspense; perfectly, luminously lit, she says nothing, expresses nothing with her body – it is black people who bodily express her desire.

This use of black people to express, to 'live', the physical dimension of Julie's life is found throughout the film, most notably after her manipulations have gone awry to the point that one of her old flames, Buck (George Brent), is about to duel with Pres's brother. The black plantation workers have gathered at the house to entertain the white guests ('a quaint old custom down here', says Julie to Pres's new, and Northern, wife, Amy). As they arrive they sing a song about marrying, heard over shots of Julie, a bitterly ironic counterpoint. She shushes the chorus and tells them to start singing, 'Gonna Raise a Ruckus To-night', then goes to the edge of the verandah and sits down, beckoning the black children to gather close round her, before joining in with the singing. The song is a jolly one and the shots of the black singers show them in happy-go-lucky Sambo style, but the last shot of the sequence closes on Julie, near to tears against the sound of this cheerful singing. The power of the sequence does not come from this ironic counterpoint alone but also from the way that Julie, by merging as nearly as possible with the singers and joining in the song, is able to express her pent-up feelings of frustration, anger, jealousy and fear, feelings for which there is no white mode of expression, which can only be lived through blacks.

The point of *Jezebel* is not that whites are different from blacks but that whites live by different rules. Unlike the two women with whom she is compared, her aunt and Amy, Julie cannot be 'white'. It is her aunt and Amy who confirm that whites are calm, controlled, rational; Julie transgresses, but in the process reveals white calm as an imposition, a form of repression of life. The film's ambivalence lies in its being a vehicle for Davis. She/Julie is a 'Jezebel', a byword for female wickedness, but none the less a star with a huge female following and shot here with the kind of radiance and glow Hollywood reserved for its favoured women stars. There is no doubt that what Julie does is wicked and that her punishment is to be understood as richly deserved; but there is also no doubt that

she is to be adored and precisely, as I've tried to argue, because she does
not conform to notions of white womanhood.

NIGHT OF THE LIVING DEAD

If blacks have more 'life' than whites, then it must follow that whites have
more 'death' than blacks. This thought has seldom been explored so
devastatingly as in the living dead films directed by George Romero –
Night of the Living Dead (1969), *Dawn of the Dead* (1978) and *Day of the
Dead* (1985).

The *Dead* films are unusual among horror films for the explicitness of
their political allegory and unique for having as their heroes 'positive' black
men. In general, the latter have been applauded merely as an instance of
affirmative action, casting colour blind a black man in a part which could
equally well have gone to a white actor. As Robin Wood notes, however,
'it is not true that [their] colour is arbitrary and without meaning'; Ben's
blackness in *Night* is used 'to signify his difference from the other characters, to set him apart from their norms' (1986a: 116), while Peter's in *Dawn*
again indicates 'his separation from the norms of white-dominated society
and his partial exemption from its constraints' (ibid.: 120). In all three
films, it is significant that the hero is a black man, and not just because this
makes him 'different' but because it makes it possible to see that whites are
the living dead. I shall confine detailed discussion here to the first film of
the trilogy.

All the dead in *Night* are whites. In a number of places, the film shows
that living whites are like, or can be mistaken for, the dead. The radio
states that the zombies are 'ordinary looking people', and the first one we
see in the film does look in the distance like some ordinary old white guy
wandering about the cemetery, somehow menacing, yet not obviously
abnormal. John, the brother in the opening sequence, recalls pretending to
be something scary to frighten Barb when they visited the graveyard as
children; he imitates the famous zombie voice of Boris Karloff to scare her
now. Halfway through the film, Barb becomes catatonic, like a dead
person. The other developed white characters emerge from where they
have been hiding, 'buried' in the cellar. Towards the end of the film, there
is an aerial shot from the point of view of a helicopter involved in the
destruction of the zombies; it looks down on a straggling line of people
moving forward uncertainly but inexorably, in exactly the same formation
as earlier shots of the zombies. It is only with a cut to a ground level shot
that we realize this is a line of vigilantes, not zombies.

Living and dead whites are indistinguishable, and the zombies' sole
raison d'être, to attack and eat the living, has resonances with the behaviour of the living whites. The vigilantes shoot and destroy the zombies with
equanimity ('Beat 'em or burn 'em – they go up pretty good', says their

leader, Chief McLelland), finally including the living – the hero, Ben (Duane Jones) – in their single-minded operations. Brother John torments Barb while living, and consumes her when he is dead. Helen and Harry Cooper bicker and snipe constantly, until their dead daughter Carrie first destroys, then eats them. The young couple, Tom and Judy, destined generically to settle down at the end of the film, instead go up in flames through Tom's stupidity and Judy's paralysed response to danger.

If whiteness and death are equated, both are further associated with the USA. That the film can be taken as a metaphor for the United States is established right at the start of the film. It opens on a car driving through apparently unpopulated back roads suggesting the road tradition of 1950s and 1960s US culture, the novel *On the Road* (1957) and the film *Easy Rider* (1969) with its idea of the 'search for America'. When the car reaches the graveyard (the USA?), a Stars and Stripes flag flutters in the foreground. The house in which the characters take shelter is archetypally middle, backwoods North American – a white wooden structure, with lace curtains, cut-glass ornaments, chintz armchairs. It, too, is immediately associated with death, in a series of shock cuts from Barb, exploring the house, to stuffed animal heads hung on the walls. Casting further heightens the all-Americanness of these zombie-like living whites. Barb is ultra-blonde and pale, and her name surely suggests the USA's best-selling doll; John is a preppy type, clean cut with straight fair hair, a white shirt with pens in the pocket, straight out of a Brooks Brothers advertisement. Judy too is dazzlingly blonde, though Tom and the Coopers are more nondescript whites.

What finally forces home the specifically white dimension of these zombie–US links are the ways in which the zombies can be destroyed. The first recalls the liberal critique of whites as ruled by their heads; as the radio announcer says, 'Kill the brain and you kill the ghoul' since, it seems, zombies/whites are nothing but their brains. The film diverges from earlier representations of the black/white, life/death opposition by representing Ben's 'life' quality in terms of practical skill, rather than innate qualities of 'being'. Particularly striking is a scene in which Ben talks about what they need to do as he dismantles a table to make boards for the windows, while Barb takes the lace cloth from it, folds and cradles it, hanging on uselessly to this token of white gentility while Ben tries to ensure their survival.

The alternative way of destroying the zombies is burning. Some of the imagery, particularly the molotov cocktails going up around empty cars, seems to recall, in its grainy black-and-white texture, newspaper coverage of the ghetto uprisings of the late 1960s, and the 'fire', as an image of Black Power's threat to white people, had wide currency (most notably in the title of James Baldwin's 1963 novel *The Fire Next Time*). The zombies are scared of light as well as fire, and Ben is associated with both, not only because of his skill in warding off the zombies with torches, but in the way he is introduced into the film. Barb wanders out of the house into the glare of a car's headlights, out of which Ben seems to emerge; a shot of the lights glaring into the camera is followed by another with Ben moving into the frame, his white shirt first, then his black face filling the frame in front of the light, in a reversal of the good/bad, white/black, light/darkness antinomies of western culture.

The film ends with the white vigilantes (indistinguishable from the zombies, remember) killing Ben, the representative of life in the film. Much of the imagery of *Night* carries over into *Dawn*, despite their many differences (most notably the latter's strong vein of humour). The opening sequence has white militia gleefully destroying living blacks and Hispanics who refuse to leave their tenement homes during the zombie emergency; as in *Night*, the black hero, Peter (Ken Foree), emerges from the light (this time from behind a white sheet with strong, bright light flooded unnaturalistically behind it); it is his practical skills that enable him to survive, skills that only the white woman, Fran (Gaylen Ross), is ultimately able to emulate. Zombieness is still linked with whiteness, even though some of the dead are black or Hispanic – a black zombie who attacks a living black man in the tenement is whited up, the colour contrast between the two emphasized in a shot of the whitened black zombie biting the living black man's neck; in the shopping mall, an overt symbol of the US way of life, editing rhymes the zombies with the shop mannequins, all of whom are white.

Day extends the critique of US values to the military–industrial complex, with its underpinnings in masculine supremacy. As Robin Wood (1986b) argues, the white men and the zombies alike are characterized by 'the conditioned reflex', the application to human affairs of relentless rationality; the scientist, Logan, teaches one of the zombies to be human again, which in practice means killing the military leader, Rhodes, out of atavistic loyalty to Logan. When Logan earlier tells Rhodes that what he is teaching the zombies is 'civility', to make them like the living, there is a sudden cut to a sequence of the men gleefully, sadistically corralling the zombies to be specimens for Logan's crazed experiments. The whiteness of all this is pointed, as before, by the presence of a black character, John (Terry Alexander), who is even more dissociated from both zombies and white male values than were Ben and Peter in the earlier films. He is not only black but West Indian, and he offers the idea of finding an island as the only hope for the two white characters (a WASP woman, Sarah, and an Irish man, Billy) not irrevocably implicated in white male values. He and Billy are not only socially marginal but also live separately from the soldiers and scientists, having set up a mock home together in the outer reaches of the underground bunker they all share. All the other living characters are redneck males, and although there is a power struggle between them, they are both more like each other and like the zombies than they are like John, Sarah or Billy. At the end of one scene, where Rhodes has established his authority over Logan, there is a final shot of John, who has looked on saying nothing; he rubs the corner of his mouth with his finger ironically, then smiles sweetly at Rhodes, an expression of ineffably insolent refusal of the white boys' games.

The *Dead* films are of course horror movies and there is a danger, as Pete Boss has pointed out, that the kind of political readings that I and others have given them may not be easy 'to integrate . . . with the fantasies of physical degradation and vulnerability' characteristic of the contemporary horror film (1986: 18). However, the use of 'body horror' in the *Dead* films to represent whiteness is not simply symbolism, making use of what happens to the genre's current conventions. On the contrary, body horror is the horror of whiteness and the films' gory pleasures are like an inverted reprise of the images of whiteness that are touched on in *Simba* and *Jezebel*.

The point about Ben, Peter and John is that in their different ways they all have control over their bodies, are able to use them to survive, know how to do things with them. The white characters (with the exception of Fran, Sarah and Billy) lose that control while alive, and come back in the monstrously uncontrolled form of zombiness. The hysterical boundedness of the white body is grotesquely transgressed as whites/zombies gouge out living white arms, pull out organs, munch at orifices. The spectre of white loss of control is evoked by the way the zombies stumble and dribble in their inexorable quest for blood, often with intestines spilling out or severed limbs dangling. White over-investment in the brain is mercilessly undermined as brains spatter agains the wall and zombies flop to the ground. 'The fear of one's own body, of how one controls it and relates to it' (Brophy 1986: 8) and the fear of not being able to control other bodies, those bodies whose exploitation is so fundamental to capitalist economy, are both at the heart of whiteness. Never has this horror been more deliriously evoked than in these films of the *Dead*.

Because my aim has been to open up an area of investigation, I shall not even attempt a rounded conclusion. Instead, let me start off again on another tack, suggested by the passing references to light and colour above. I suspect that there is some very interesting work to be done on the invention of photography and the development of lighting codes in relation to the white face, which results in the technicist ideology that one sometimes hears of it being 'more difficult' to photograph black people. Be that as it may, it is the case that the codes of glamour lighting in Hollywood were developed in relation to white women, to endow them with a glow and radiance that has correspondences with the transcendental rhetoric of popular Christianity.

Of no woman star was this more true than Marilyn Monroe, known by the press at the time as 'the Body'. I've argued elsewhere that her image is an inescapably and necessarily white one (1986: 42–5); in many of her films this combines with the conventions of glamour lighting to make her disappear as flesh and blood even more thoroughly than is the case with other women stars. Her first appearance in *The Seven Year Itch* (1955), for instance, is a classic instance of woman as spectacle caught in a shot from the male protagonist's point of view. It opens on Richard (Tom Ewell), on his hands and knees on the floor looking for something, bottom sticking up, a milk bottle between his legs – the male body shown, as is routine in sex comedies, as ludicrously grotesque; he hears the door-bell and opens the door to his flat; as the door opens light floods in on him; he looks and there is a cut to the hall doorway, where the curvy shape of a woman is visible through the frosted glass. The woman's shape is placed exactly within the frame of the door window, the doorway is at the end of the hall, exactly in the centre of the frame; a set of enclosing rectangles create a strong sense of perspective, and emphasize the direction of Richard's/our gaze. The colouring of the screen is pinky-white and light emanates from behind the doorway where the woman is. All we see of her is her silhouette, defining her proportions, but she also looks translucent. The film cuts back to Richard, his jaw open in awe, bathed in stellar light. Later in the film, when the Monroe character's tomato plant crashes on to Richard's patio, we have another shot of her from Richard's point of view. He looks up, and there is a cut to Monroe looking down from her balcony, apparently nude; the wall behind her is dark, as is the vegetation on the balcony, so her face and shoulders stand out as white. Such moments conflate unreal angel-glow with sexual aura.

The Seven Year Itch is a very smart film. Through innumerable gags and cross-references, it lets on that it knows about male fantasy and its remote relation to reality. Yet it is also part of the Monroe industry, peddling an impossible dream, offering another specifically white ideal as if it embodies all heterosexual male yearning, offering another white image that dissolves in the light of its denial of its own specificity.

White women are constructed as the apotheosis of desirability, all that a man could want, yet nothing that can be had, nor anything that a woman can be. But, as I have argued, white representation *in general* has this everything-and-nothing quality.

Screen, 29 (4) (1988)

NOTES

1 Made by Tony Dowmunt, Maris Clark, Rooney Martin and Kobena Mercer for Albany Video, London.
2 See also the arguments about feminism and ethnicity in Carby 1982.

3 This restrictive definition of racism has been disputed by, among others, Hall 1980.

REFERENCES

Banton, Michael (1977) *The Idea of Race*, London: Tavistock.
Bhabha, Homi K. (1983) 'The Other Question – the Stereotype and Colonial Discourse', *Screen* 24 (6): 18–36.
Boss, Pete (1986) 'Vile Bodies and Bad Medicine', *Screen* 27 (1): 14–25.
Brophy, Philip (1986) 'Horrality – the Textuality of Contemporary Horror Films', *Screen* 27 (1): 2–13.
Carby, Hazel (1982) 'White Woman Listen! Black Feminism and the Boundaries of Sisterhood', in Centre for Contemporary Cultural Studies (ed.) *The Empire Strikes Back*, London: Hutchinson, 212–23.
Chodorow, Nancy (1978) *The Reproduction of Mothering*, Berkeley: University of California Press.
Cripps, Thomas (1977) *Slow Fade to Black*, New York: Oxford University Press.
Dyer, Richard (1986) *Heavenly Bodies*, London: Macmillan.
Dyer, Richard (1992) 'The Role of Stereoypes', Chapter 3 above.
Fanon, Frantz (1986) *Black Skin, White Mask*, London: Pluto.
Fisher, Lucy (ed.) (1992) *Imitation of Life*, New Brunswick: Rutgers University Press.
Fredrickson, George (1972) *The Black Image in the White Mind*, New York: Harper & Row.
Fryer, Peter (1984) *Staying Power*, London: Pluto.
Gilman, Sandor L. (1985) *Pathology and Difference*, Ithaca, NY: Cornell University Press.
Gilroy, Paul (1987) *There Ain't No Black in the Union Jack*, London: Hutchinson.
Hall, Stuart (1980) 'Race, Articulation and Societies Structured in Dominance', in UNESCO *Sociological Theories: Race and Colonialism*, Paris: UNESCO.
Hall, Stuart (1981) 'The Whites of their Eyes', in George Bridges and Rosalind Brunt (eds) *Silver Linings*, London: Lawrence & Wishart, 28–52.
Haskell, Molly (1974) *From Reverence to Rape*, New York: Holt, Rinehart & Winston.
Hill, John (1986) *Sex, Class and Realism in British Cinema*, London: British Film Institute.
Jordan, Winthrop (1969) *White over Black*, Harmondsworth: Penguin.
Lawrence, Errol (1982) 'In the Abundance of Water the Fool is Thirsty: Sociology and Black Pathology', in Centre for Contemporary Cultural Studies (ed.) *The Empire Strikes Back*, London: Hutchinson, 95–142.
Lewis, David Levering (1981) *When Harlem Was in Vogue*, New York: Knopf.
Mannin, Ethel (1930) *Confessions and Impressions*, New York: Doubleday Doran.
Marcuse, Herbert (1964) *One Dimensional Man*, Boston: Beacon Press.
Medhurst, Andy (1986) 'Dirk Bogarde', in Charles Barr (ed.) *All Our Yesterdays*, London: British Film Institute, 346–54.
Neale, Steve (1979/80) 'The Same Old Story', *Screen Education* 32/3: 33–8.
Parry, Benita (1987) 'Problems in Current Theories of Colonial Discourse', *Oxford Literary Review* 9 (1/2): 27–58.
Perkins, T. E. (1979) 'Rethinking Stereotypes', in Michèle Barrett, Philip Corrigan, Annette Kuhn and Janet Wolff (eds) *Representation and Cultural Practice*, London: Croom Helm, 135–59.
Pines, Jim (1975) *Blacks in Films*, London: Studio Vista.

Robinson, Cedric (1983) *Black Marxism*, London: Zed Books.

Saïd, Edward (1978) *Orientalism*, London: Routledge & Kegan Paul.

Thompson, John O. (1978) 'Screen Acting and the Commutation Test', *Screen* 19 (2): 55–70.

Wood, Robin (1986a) *Hollywood from Vietnam to Reagan*, New York: Columbia University Press.

Wood, Robin (1986b) 'The Woman's Nightmare: Masculinity in *The Day of the Dead*', *CineAction!* 6: 45–9.

FURTHER READING

Blackburn, Julia (1979) *The White Men: The First Response of Aboriginal People to the White Man*, London: Orbis.

Bruckner, Pascal (1983) *Les Sanglots de l'homme blanc*, Paris: Editions du Seuil.

Frye, Marilyn (1983) 'On Being White', in *The Politics of Reality*, Trumansburg, NY: The Crossing Press.

hooks, bell (1991) 'Representing Whiteness: Seeing Wings of Desire', in *Yearning: Race, Gender and Cultural Politics*, London: Turnaround, 165–72.

—— (1992) 'Representations of Whiteness', in *Black Looks: Race and Representation*, Boston: South End Press, 165–78.

Malbert, Roger and Coates, Julia (1991) *Exotic Europeans*, London: South Bank Centre.

Malcolmson, Scott L. (1991) 'Heart of Whiteness', *Voice Literary Supplement*, March: 10–14.

Michaels, Walter Benn (1988) 'The Souls of White Folk', in Elaine Scarry (ed.) *Literature and the Body: Essays on Populations and Persons*, Baltimore: Johns Hopkins University Press, 185–209.

Roediger, David (1991) *The Wages of Whiteness*, London: Verso.

Saxton, Alexander (1990) *The Rise and Fall of the White Republic*, London: Verso.

Ware, Vron (1992) *Beyond the Pale: White Women, Racism and History*, London: Verso.

Index